IMPERIAL CONTROL OF THE ADMINISTRATION OF JUSTICE IN THE THIRTEEN AMERICAN COLONIES, 1684–1776

BY

GEORGE ADRIAN WASHBURNE, Ph.D.

Assistant Professor of European History, Ohio State Univsrsity

THE LAWBOOK EXCHANGE, LTD.

Clark, New Jersey

ISBN 9781584776215 (hardcover)
ISBN 9781616192501 (paperback)

Lawbook Exchange edition 2012

The quality of this reprint is equivalent to the quality of the original work.

THE LAWBOOK EXCHANGE, LTD.
33 Terminal Avenue
Clark, New Jersey 07066-1321

Please see our website for a selection of our other publications and fine facsimile reprints of classic works of legal history:
www.lawbookexchange.com

Library of Congress Cataloging-in-Publication Data

Washburne, George Adrian, 1884-1948.
Imperial control of the administration of justice in the thirteen American colonies, 1684-1776 / George Adrian Washburne.
p. cm.
Originally published: New York : Columbia University, 1923. (Studies in history, economics, and public law ; no. 238)
Thesis (Ph.D.)--Columbia University, 1923.
Includes bibliographical references and index.
ISBN 1-58477-621-8 (alk. paper)
1. Justice, Administration of--United States--History. 2. United States--Politics and government--To 1775. 3. Great Britain. Privy Council--History. 4. Great Britain--Colonies--Administration--History. I. Title. II. Series: Studies in history, economics, and public law ; no. 238.

KF8700.A45W37 2005
25'.341'0973--dc22 2005016079

Printed in the United States of America on acid-free paper

STUDIES IN HISTORY, ECONOMICS AND PUBLIC LAW

EDITED BY THE FACULTY OF POLITICAL SCIENCE OF
COLUMBIA UNIVERSITY

Volume CV] [Number 2

Whole Number 238

IMPERIAL CONTROL OF THE ADMINISTRATION OF JUSTICE IN THE THIRTEEN AMERICAN COLONIES, 1684–1776

BY

GEORGE ADRIAN WASHBURNE, Ph.D.

Assistant Professor of European History, Ohio State Univsrsity

New York
COLUMBIA UNIVERSITY
SELLING AGENTS
New York; Longmans, Green & Co.
London: P. S. King & Son Ltd.

PREFACE

IMPERIAL relations will always be a subject of interest to students of the expansion of Europe. Problems of administration connected with the control of the original thirteen American dependencies are of interest to students of American history. Of these problems of administration between Great Britain and her colonies there are none more important than the one concerning the control of the developing legal system in the new world. With this phase of imperial administration this study is concerned.

The English government had evolved by the beginning of the eighteenth century the idea of a concrete, constructive policy with regard to the administration of justice in the thirteen American colonies. Not only was the English system to be established but in cases in which variations had occurred in the colonial development, these were to be moulded to conform with the accepted, traditional, Anglo-Saxon pattern so venerated in England. The Board of Trade, as early as 1700, asked for a report from all the dependencies concerning legal usage, looking toward a plan of standardization with the English system as a model. That this plan was not carried to its logical conclusion by the development of a uniform system was due to the fact that the immediate problems of the eighteenth century, particularly that of imperial defense, pressed so closely upon the home government that the administration of justice had to be controlled through judicial agencies already functioning. In this connection the King in Council as a court of last resort in the appellate system from the colonies became the important restraining and correcting influence. Through this agency the home government not only suggested technical procedure in the colonial courts but reviewed and passed upon the principal colonial problems of the day. An attempt has been made to show in broad outline the development of this administrative system.

This study was begun some years ago at the suggestion of Profesor H. L. Osgood of Columbia University. His unfailing kindness, warm sympathy and scholarly counsel were never more in evidence than at the time this study was in preparation. The removal of his guiding hand by death meant a loss which has been deeply felt.

Indebtedness must be expressed to other teachers and friends. Professor William A. Dunning encouraged and aided in many ways the preparation of this work. Professor Dixon Ryan Fox and Professor R. L. Schuyler of Columbia University gave much of their time to a close examination of the manuscript and made helpful and stimulating suggestions for which the utmost gratitude is expressed. In no less a sense there is indebtedness to Professor W. H. Siebert and Profesor E. H. McNeal of the Ohio State University who read this study carefully and whose suggestions have been embodied in it. Thanks are also due to Professor W. R. Shepherd and Dr. H. E. Yntema of Columbia University and Professor A. H. Tuttle of the Ohio State University.

Many kindnesses and courtesies were shown by the officials in charge of libraries and collections of manuscripts. The patience and untiring effort of the attendants at the Public Record Office, London, England, should be particularly mentioned. There was also a courteous attitude shown at the British Museum, the Library of the Pennsylvania Historical Society, Congressional Library in Washington, the Columbia University Library and the Ohio State University Library. Special thanks are due Miss Maude Jeffrey, reference librarian at the Ohio State University Library, for her kindness in the matter of interlibrary loans.

G. A. W.

Ohio State University,
September, 1922

CONTENTS

PAGE

CHAPTER II

The King in Council

PAGE

CHAPTER III

Appeals to the King in Council—1684-1745

CHAPTER IV

Appeals to the King in Council—1745–1776

CHAPTER V

The Working of the Imperial System

CHAPTER I

Imperial Development of a Colonial Legal System

When England began her expansion she had no definite idea of developing a colonial empire. Consequently control of the colonies that later grew up was a mixture of ancient English custom and tradition with an attitude constantly changing to meet the exigencies of the moment. The first grants of the English government with regard to commerce and the establishment of trading-posts recognized the fact that the adventurers were English subjects and should be bound by English law.[1] All enactments made by them were to be of such kind that they would not be repugnant to English law. Offenders might be punished by fine and imprisonment. These statements sounded the key note from which the provisions of the other charters were taken. As the colonies gradually began to develop, it was assumed that the organization of local courts in accordance with English custom lay in the hands of the governor and council. Along with this it was taken for granted that appeal from the colonial courts to the King in Council was inherently the right of each English subject.[2]

Within the colonies the imperial system attempted a control and regulation of judicial matters by five different

[1] *Vide* patent to Gilbert, 1578, charter to Raleigh, March 25, 1584, and particularly the East India Company charter, December 31, 1600.

[2] There are numerous instances of the truth of this statement throughout the published acts of the Privy Council. *Vide Acts Privy Council, Colonial Series, passim.*

methods. These methods of control were: first, by the charters which ordinarily defined the general legal rights; second, by the commissions and instructions from the home government to the governors of the different provinces; third, by the constant activity of the Board of Trade, after its creation in 1696—particularly, the development by this organization in 1700 of the idea of a constructive policy to mould the judicial system to one standard; fourth, by a review of colonial legislation and the disallowance of such provincial law as did not conform to the accepted English legal system, and finally, by the correction of irregularities in court procedure by the decision of the King in Council when such irregularities were detected in cases brought on appeal to the home government.

The charters of the various colonies defined the legal rights of the inhabitants. They all contained clauses modeled upon the old idea of the earlier charters that all adventurers and settlers were to be considered English subjects with, as specifically stated in the first charter of Virginia, "all liberties, franchises and immunities within any of our other dominions, to all intents and purposes as if they had been abiding and born, within this our realm of England or any other of our said Dominions."[3] The idea that no law should be made by legislative bodies of the colonies in conflict with established English law was repeated again and again.[1] Usually a general statement covered the whole administration of justice, but in the later charters the wording became more definite and after 1664 appeal to the King in Council was mentioned.

In the early charters the judicial administration was given along with the legislative duties to the central authority of

[1] McDonald, *Select Charters Illustrative of American History*, p. 8.

[2] Charters to Virginia, 1606, 1609, 1612; First Charter to Massachusetts 1629. McDonald, *Charters*, pp. 8, 14, 19, 41.

the colony. Lord Baltimore had the power to constitute and to ordain judges and justices and to pardon offenses as well as "to do all and singular other things belonging to the completion of justice in all actions, suits, causes and matters whatsoever as well criminal as personal, real and mixed."[1] The grant to the Duke of York in 1664, besides giving him the usual right to erect courts, reserved to the crown the right of the "receiving, hearing and determining of the appeal and appeals of all or any person or persons of, in, or belonging to the Territories or Islands aforesaid in or touching any judgment or sentences to be there made or given."[2] The grant to William Penn in 1681 gave him the right to appoint judges, justices, magistrates and officers and arrange all things for the complete establishment of justice; but reserved the rights of "receiving, hearing and determining the appeal and appeals of all or any person or persons of, in, or belonging to the Territories aforesaid or touching any judgment to be there made or given."[3]

The famous 1691 charter to Massachusetts indicated the eighteenth century attitude toward administrative justice in the colonies. Here the King in Council was named as the court of last resort in cases wherein the matter in difference exceeded the value of 300 pounds sterling and when the suits were personal actions. Moreover the appeal had to be made within fourteen days after the judgment had been rendered, security had to be given by the party or parties appealing, as well as by the party suing or taking out execution to make restitution in case the judgment of the inferior court should be reversed or annulled, and no execution was to be stayed or suspended by reason of the appeal.[4]

[1] McDonald, *Charters*, p. 57.

[2] *Ibid.*, p. 138.

[3] *Ibid.*, pp. 186-187.

[4] *CO5/860*, no. 58, enclosure ii, extract of Charters of Mass. Bay.

By inference from the general statements of the rights of the colonists as Englishmen, as well as by direct mention of appeal and judicial administration, the charters sought to erect a legal system. But whether the charters stated it definitely or not, the attitude of all the agencies of the English government was that it was the inherent right of any of "His Majesty's subjects to appeal directly to the King."[1]

The commissions and instructions to the governors of the royal colonies were explicit both as to the formation of inferior courts and their procedure as well as to the rules and methods under which appeals were to be approved. By tradition the king was "the fountain of justice" and the governor in the colony was his representative. By his commission the governor was empowered to erect courts of justice. As a result of the general obligation to maintain courts and enforce the law he had the appointment of judicial officers. At first this power of appointment together with that of removal was unlimited, but later the judges and justices of the peace were appointed by the governor with the consent of the council.[2] The early instructions gave the governor power to appoint, and stated that removals were not to be made without just cause. Later the home government insisted definitely upon an appointment upon the basis of tenure during pleasure only.[3]

As we shall see, this led to opposition on the part of the

[1] *Board of Trade Journal,* vol. xii, CO391/12, p. 195; *Calendar of State Papers, Colonial Series,* vol. xii, no. 315; *Acts Privy Council, Colonial Series,* vol. ii, no. 733.

[2] *North Carolina Records,* vol. iii, p. 70; *ibid.,* p. 102. The commission to Burrington gives the general power of appointment, while the instructions limit it and further prohibit the erection of any special court without order from the home government.

[3] *North Carolina Records,* vol. v, p. 1107; instructions to Dobbs of North Carolina. Greene, *Provincial Governor,* p. 135.

colonies which attempted to insist upon the holding of judicial offices on the basis of tenure during good behavior. Although the commissions and instructions gave the governor the right to erect courts, the practice in the different colonies varied, and legislative acts of the assemblies established and organized courts.[1] The theory remained that the right to erect courts remained with the crown, but the home government seems at times to have recognized actions of the assemblies in this respect.[2]

The instructions to the governors also indicated the circumstances under which appeals might be granted to the King in Council. In the instructions to Governor Sloughter of New York in 1690 the minimum amount which could receive attention in case of fines for misdemeanors was fixed at two hundred pounds.[3] Later in 1709 this was repeated in the instructions to General Robert Hunter of the same province.[4] This seems to have been the usual amount decided upon by the home government but as low an amount as one hundred pounds was mentioned in the instructions to Burrington as governor of North Carolina.[5] This determination of amount seems to have grown out of a sincere desire on the part of the home government to protect the individual from injustice at the hands of the colonial officials. In the same way the instructions indicated that there were complaints concerning delay of justice and other

[1] Hening, *Statutes of Virginia*, iii, pp. 95, 287-302; *North Carolina Records*, vol. iv, p. 337.

[2] *New Jersey Documents*, vol. iii, p. 322; Greene, *Provincial Governor*, p. 139.

[3] *New York Documents*, vol. iii, pp. 685-691.

[4] *New York Documents*, vol. v, pp. 124-143.

[5] *North Carolina Records*, vol. iii, p. 90. *Vide* also instructions to Dobbs of North Carolina, *North Carolina Records*, vol. v, p. 1107. The question of the relation of the governor to the judiciary is discussed in Greene, *Provincial Governor*, chapter vii.

irregularities and insisted upon a careful oversight of all judicial matters.

The Board of Trade after its creation in 1696 was besieged with documents asking that irregularities that had developed in the judicial matters of the colonies might receive the attention of the home government. The complaints came largely from Massachusetts, Rhode Island and Connecticut; occasionally protests came from the other colonies. The demand for an investigation reached white heat in 1699.

There was considerable dissatisfaction in Connecticut which grew out of the famous Palmes case. John and Nicholas Hallam, together with Edward Palmes, had been refused the right of appeal from that colony. The Privy Council, upon petition of these Connecticut men, had taken the matter in hand and had referred it to the Board of Trade. The Board reported that the King "might fitly require the Government and Company of the Colony to take care that no such obstruction be allowed, but that all cases upon differences between man and man about private rights be fairly heard and judged by the proper methods of the courts established in that colony." This statement added that it was the inherent right of the King "to receive and determine appeals" from all his subjects in America. The attitude thus expressed by the Board was incorporated in the order in council of March 9, 1699, stating the imperial position with regard to appeals.[1] Connecticut took a determined stand upon what she considered her rights and the case gave the Board no little trouble.[2] The Board wrote letters to the colony concerning the matter and received several memorials and reports setting forth the colony's side

[1] *Acts Privy Council, Colonial Series*, vol. ii, no. 733, p. 328; *Calendar State Papers*, vol. xii, no. 160.

[2] *CO391/12, Board of Trade Journal*, vol. xii, pp. 12, 39; *CO5/1287*.

of the case.[1] Mr. Wharton, the attorney who was handling the case, finally reported March 7, 1700, that the governor and company of Connecticut had no regard for the order in council of March 9, 1699, which had ordered the colony to admit the appeal. The Board took up the matter with Wharton in person on the Friday following this report.[2] The result of this conference was a letter from the Board of Trade to Connecticut under date of April 4, 1700. Connecticut did not respond promptly and Wharton reported that the delay "was evident argument of their (the governor and company of Connecticut) declining to allow Palmes' appeal as they had been directed to do".[3] The colony, however, did draw up an energetic statement of its position and forwarded it to Sir Henry Ashurst, the colonial agent in England, who stated the attitude of Connecticut to the Board.[4]

In Rhode Island, Francis Brinley had complained of the obstruction of justice in that colony and had brought the matter of colonial judicial procedure to the attention of the Privy Council, which had referred the matter to the Board of Trade.[5] A vigorous letter was sent to the governor and company of Rhode Island restating the principle that appeal was the inherent right of Englishmen.[6] In November, 1699, the Earl of Bellomont thought fit to report to the Board irregularities in Rhode Island.[7] The Board de-

[1] *Board of Trade Journal,* vol. xiii, p. 54.

[2] *Ibid.,* p. 34.

[3] *Ibid.,* p. 52.

[4] *Ibid.,* pp. 265, 274, 288. The colonial statement is under date of December 5, 1700.

[5] *Acts Privy Council, Colonial Series,* vol. ii, no. 732; *Calendar State Papers,* vol. xii, no. 122.

[6] *Board of Trade Journal,* vol. xii, pp. 9-10, 25; *CO5/1287; Board of Trade Journal,* vol. xiv, p. 412.

[7] Earl of Bellomont to Board of Trade, November 27, 1699. *Board of Trade Journal,* vol. xiv, p. 344.

cided at its next meeting to draw up a representation to the King setting forth the general state of affairs in the colony.[1]

A memorial from one Christopher Almy of Portsmouth, Rhode Island, had come to the Board in 1700. This also stated irregularities in court procedure.[2] Almy had been impaneled on the grand jury in a trial held in Newport, March 26, 1700. A bill of indictment had been preferred by one John Pocock against a Joseph Pembert of Westerly for maliciously speaking at a town meeting in such a way as to arouse seditious feeling against the government. Like indictments were preferred against John Lewis and Edward Blevin. The grand jury could not find that any law had been violated or that anything had been done which would show contempt for the existing government. The court was, however, not satisfied. Three persons were added to the jury of twelve and the court "sent them forth again who after debate returned the same decision." Then the court added six more to the jury and "required them to go forth a third time". This time after some debate twelve of the twenty-one agreed to return the verdict desired by the court while nine, of whom Almy was one, held to the first verdict. The memorial further recited that the bills were delivered into court, not signed by the grand jury as should have been the case but indorsed by the clerk with the statement, "received by the Court, Wilson Clarke, clerk" and underneath in the same handwriting these words, "a true bill." At the trial later the verdict of not guilty was brought in twice but each time the court "turned out" the jurors and the third time after a strict charge to bring in the verdict of guilty this was done by the jury.[3] However un-

[1] *Board of Trade Journal*, vol. xiv, p. 367.

[2] *CO5/1260*, no. 417.

[3] "An account upon Oath of Mr. Hearne of the proceedings at a Court of Tryall held in Newport on Rhode Island, March 26, 1700." *CO5/1260*, no. 417.

usual this memorial may have been, it served the purpose, with the Brinley case, of making the members of the Board of Trade think that improper things were being done in the name of justice in Rhode Island.

In Virginia there was dissatisfaction with the process of judicial administration. A memorial was presented to the Board in 1697 showing the state of affairs in that province.[1] This showed that there had been a lack of understanding before 1680 as to what constituted the duties of the general assembly in its relation to the judiciary. The assembly had been in the habit of hearing appeals from the general court. Lord Culpepper had brought this matter to the attention of the home government. According to the attitude which we know was developing, the appellate jurisdiction of the general assembly was abolished as contrary to the laws of England and cases could be appealed only when they involved a value of 300 pounds and security had been given to defray costs and damages. The memorial complained of the arbitrary attitude of the governor in judicial matters. The governor gave commissions to gentlemen in the counties to act as justices of the peace; these commissions he renewed each year in order, as it was claimed, to get fees and secure further influence. The county courts were badly managed by men of little education and this was particularly felt after the first stock of Virginia gentlemen was gone. There was, therefore, great need of means by which cases might be reviewed and it was considered a grievance that there was no means of redress for a litigant, except "the practically limitless expense of carrying his case to Whitehall which few in Virginia had the purse or skill to manage." Complaint was also made in this memorial of the proceedings of the courts; the process was in many cases repugnant to

[1] *Calendar State Papers, Colonial Series,* vol. x, no. 650; October 20, 1697.

the laws of England and considered by the colonists as irregular. The selection of juries was illegally made, the sheriff returning juries summoned without authority from places remote from that in which the contested act had occurred. All these irregularities in Virginia the memorial wished to bring to the attention of the home government.[1]

From Maryland Governor Blackiston had written the Board of Trade wishing to know whether appeals from Maryland in admiralty cases should be made to the High Court of Admiralty in England in pursuance of the commission issued by that court for erecting vice-admiralty courts in Maryland.[2] The Board of Trade was in doubt as to what should be done, and ordered that Lord Baltimore's patent for Maryland be examined to see whether anything therein might have relation to the question in hand. The Blakiston letter was sent to the attorney and solicitor general and a copy to Sir Charles Hedges, who had been judge of the English admiralty court since 1689, for their opinions.[3] The attorney general reported immediately that he was of the opinion that there were express clauses both in the commission of vice admiral and in the commission to the judge of the admiralty which would allow a right of appeal from any sentence to the court of admiralty in England. Where either party thought himself aggrieved by any sentence given in the vice-admiralty court, it was his opinion, that the litigant had a right to appeal to the High Court of Admiralty in England and that such appeal must be allowed there.[4]

[1] This memorial is entitled "An Account of the Present State and Government of Virginia," is signed by Hartwell, Blair and Chilton and is dated October 20, 1697.

[2] *Board of Trade Journal,* vol. xii, p. 176. Blakiston to the Board of Trade, May 20, 1699; received by Board, Sept. 15, 1699.

[3] *Board of Trade Journal,* vol. xii, pp. 178-179.

[4] Sept. 28, 1699. *CO5/714. Calendar State Papers,* x, p. 442, no. 797.

Sir Charles Hedges answered to the same effect.[1] In answer to Governor Blakiston, the Board wrote him under date of September 20, 1699, and informed him that as to the doubt which he proposed about appeals there was no contradiction between the clauses which he had sent the Board from his commission as governor and those of the commissions issued out of the High Court of Admiralty. But, the communication concluded, if the governor found any inconvenience in pursuing the directions of each commission, as the different cases which should arise might respectively require, the Board would use "its best endeavors upon any notice that such remedies should be applied as would be though fit."[2]

In Massachusetts there had been trouble arising over the question of appeals and judicial administration. The Board of Trade had attempted to get a report from the colony and had become rather impatient over the delay encountered in the matter. This had grown out of the famous Brenton case.

Jahleel Brenton, collector and surveyor of the customs in New England, had made a seizure of the brigantine *Mary* in 1691 with her lading of tobacco. This seizure had been made because bond had not been given as the navigation laws directed. The case was brought to trial in the colonial courts and the bringantine with her cargo was adjudged as forfeited to the king. But the case was taken on appeal to the court of assistants in Boston where the former judgment was reversed. Brenton also in the same year made a seizure of iron imported contrary to law into Massachusetts from Spain. The jury in this case gave the verdict in favor of "the said iron"; the collector at once entered a review.

[1] *CO5/714*, no. 74. Sir Charles Hedges to Mr. Popple, Sept. 21, 1699.

[2] *Calendar of State Papers*, x, p. 444. Board of Trade to Governor Blakiston, Sept. 20, 1699.

The claimant in the case broke open the storehouse where the iron was kept and by force took it away. Both of these cases Brenton brought on appeal to the King in Council.

In the report of the committee to the King in Council May 27, 1697, Brenton was admitted to an appeal from the judgment given in the court of assistants in Boston with regard to the brigantine *Mary;* his appeal concerning the seizure of iron was also admitted, provided that he would give security to prosecute and abide by the King's determination. Notice was served upon the governor and council of the province of Massachusetts to transmit authentic copies of all the records and proceedings relating to these appeals under the seal of the province. It was definitely stated at this time to the Massachusetts government that "the officers of His Majesty's customs in Massachusetts Bay" were to have the right of appeal in cases of like nature. The only condition was that the usual security must be given for the prosecution of the appeals within a twelve month after the appeal had been made. Warning was also given that due care must be taken that ships and goods seized in the province were not to be discharged without due process of law.[1]

In answer to this came the so-called "New England Address about Appeals", dated March 25, 1698. In "dutiful manner, humbly" it was represented that Massachusetts could not help but observe that the order extended not only to the two cases mentioned which were tried several years previously, but that it looked forward to all cases of like nature without any limitation of value. The provisions of the charter were enumerated to show under what circumstances the crown had permitted appeals, particularly calling attention to the three hundred pound limit.[2] Then it was

[1] Report of the committee to the Lords Justices in Council, May 27, 1697; *CO5/860.*

[2] *Ibid.*

stated that under the new interpretation the people of Massachusetts were to be deprived of the privilege granted in their charter in all cases of seizures under the three hundred pound value. It was evident that much injustice and considerable hardship would be endured by the people of the province if the removal of a case could be had to the crown after the matter had passed through the courts of Massachusetts and had been tried one or more times by due methods and course of law. This would be particularly evident in the case of a removal, when no ship or goods seized for trading or for being imported into the colony contrary to law, might be discharged until final judgment had been given by the crown. The people would, it was stated, be so discouraged that in many cases of considerable value, the charge and trouble of undertaking a voyage to England and attendance there to wait the issue would be "so great and unsupportable that many would rather choose to quit claims and forego their interests than pursue the same further". As an example, the case relating to the ship, *The Two Brothers,* was cited in which the time elapsing was from September 1691 until July 1697. Besides, the memorial continued, the very great detriment and loss that would unavoidably happen to ships and goods by lying so long and possibly upon trial there, would in many instance be no just cause for the seizure, and the claimants or owners would be at much loss. If the owners should be found guilty of any transgression, the crown's interests would greatly suffer it not be utterly lost.[1] Praying for a long and prosperous reign for the king, the petition humbly asked his consideration of the privileges granted by the charter.

All the papers in the Brenton case were transmitted by William Stoughton to the Board in order that the examina-

[1] *Ibid.*

tion of the case might be thoroughly made.[1] All through July the Board attempted to deal with it and on September 26, 1699, after a reading of the representation of the Board of Trade the whole subject was referred to Lord Chief Justice Holt who was to be attended therein by the crown's attorney and solicitor general. The portion of the charter of Massachusetts having to do with appeals and the "New England Address about Appeals" were sent to them.[2]

With regard to this subject the attorney and the solicitor general had reported to the Board of Trade April 4, 1699, in answer to the inquiry of August 4, 1698, that in personal actions where the matters in question exceeded the value of three hundred pounds an appeal of right ought to be allowed by the express words of the Massachusetts charter. Also an appeal upon any action or information of seizure of ship or goods for trading contrary to the law where the value was either above or under three hundred pounds, would lie from the judgment of the court of judicature in the colony, in case His Majesty in Council should think fit to allow thereof. An allowance of such appeal would be no infringement or violation of the charter.[3] Mr. William Popple had pointed out that the real difficulty underlying the whole matter was the improbability that it could ever have been intended in the drawing of the charter that the king should thereby exclude himself from having a remedy against any unjust determination of the courts of Massachusetts in matters relating to his customs and revenue. This would inevitably be the consequence if no appeals were allowed in these matters under the value of three hundred pounds, because many small vessels and cargoes were

[1] *CO5/860*, no. 61. Wm. Stoughton to Board of Trade, July 7, 1699.

[2] *CO5/860*, no. 71, order signed by John Povey.

[3] *CO5/860*, no. 58, *Calendar State Papers*, 1699, p. 127, no. 234.

not really of that value and it might be easy for illegal traders so to order their affairs so that no single seizure should amount to this.[1] The "New England Address about Appeals" had brought out this point particularly as well as the attitude of the Massachusetts Bay Government on the subject.[2]

During 1699 the Board was still attempting to get a satisfactory adjustment with Massachusetts concerning this whole subject of administration of justice. Sir Henry Ashurst, the agent for Massachusetts, was notified that if he were not able to get a speedy answer, the Board would be obliged to request the attorney general to report the matter without his aid.[3] The latter part of June the Board was notified that Sir Henry Ashurst was busily engaged upon the matter and a letter was ordered dispatched to him urging the greatest speed.[4] Despite this agitation Massachusetts gave no satisfactory reply and the Board was obliged to come to the conclusion that her attitude was wilful disregard of the wishes of the home government. The Privy Council in May 1700 dismissed the appeal concerning Brenton's seizure of the *Mary*.[5]

During the régime of the Earl of Bellomont, he had expressed dissatisfaction with the judicial system and there was constant exchange of communications between the governor and the Board. The lord justices of England

[1] *CO5/860*, no. 58, Enclosure, Wm. Popple to Attorney General, August 4, 1698.

[2] Wm. Stoughton to Board of Trade, March 25, 1698; *CO5/860; Board of Trade Journal*, vol. xii, pp. 113, 115.

[3] *Board of Trade Journal*, vol. xii, p. 61; *CO391/12*, p. 61.

[4] *Ibid.*, p. 88, June 21, 1699.

[5] The Brenton case before the Board of Trade is given in *Board of Trade Journal*, vol. xii, p. 88 *et seq.; Acts Privy Council, Colonial Series*, vol. ii, no. 480, p. 241.

had ordered the Council of Trade to direct Lord Bellomont to take care upon his arrival in New England that the officers of the King's customs be allowed to appeal to the King in Council and that ships and goods be not discharged after seizure without due process of law.[1] From New York the Earl of Bellomont had written repeatedly to the Board requesting an able attorney general for the province in order that justice might be administered in a more satisfactory manner; and late in 1699 the Board drew up a representation to lay before the King for the necessity of such a step.[2]

As a result of this clash between the various colonies and the imperial system, the Board of Trade made a direct representation to the Privy Council looking toward a constructive policy of controlling and systematizing judicial proceedings within the provinces. In consequence of this we have the order in council of July 18, 1700, which gave solemn warning to the dependencies that the whole matter of judicial proceeding and the question of appeals were to be made the subject of an investigation by the home government. This stated:

It is this day ordered by their excellencies the Lord Justices in Council that directions be sent to the respective governors of His Majesty's Plantations in America as well such as are granted in Propriety as such as are governed by Commission from His Majesty to transmit an account to the Lords Commissioners for Trade and Plantations in the most particular manner of the method of proceedings in the several courts upon trails of all sorts of causes in the said courts in those parts and that the same be communicated by their Lordships to this Board for His Majesty's better information in determining of appeals from the plantations. And the Lord Com-

[1] *Acts Privy Council, Colonial Series*, vol. ii, p. 314, no. 682; *Calendar State Papers*, vol. x, no. 1214, p. 570.

[2] *Board of Trade Journal*, vol. xii, p. 291; *CO391/12*, p. 291.

missioners for Trade and Plantations are to signify their Excellencies' pleasure herein to the said respective governors accordingly.[1]

On August first the Board in compliance with this order in council of July 18 issued a circular letter to all the governors and governments in America relating to the method of proceeding "in the several courts upon tryalls of all sorts of causes in those parts." [2] The response from the colonies showed in theory faithful conformity to English tradition and a steady progression of appeal from the inferior courts to the King in Council.[3] And there can be no doubt that where an elaborate arrangement of the judiciary had been accomplished the courts in theory were so organized. Allowing for minor differences and other variations due to settlement and peculiarities of location, the judicial arrangements were developed according to the best English custom. So much so that the Board seemed to recognize that its future duty would be not so much to deal with the problem of conforming colonial courts to an established English system as to correct abuses which had grown up within systems already established.

The replies of the governors began to come in during the year 1701. Governor Blakiston apologized for not being more speedy in his answer, but excused himself on the ground that there had been no ship sailing for England until May 1701.[4] He then gave what he called a "scheme of the Judicial proceedings in Maryland both Criminal and

[1] *CO324/7*, no. 35; *CO323/3*, no. 75; *Acts Privy Council, Colonial Series*, vol. ii, no. 797, p. 356; *Calendar State Papers*, xiii, no. 651.

[2] *CO324/7*, pp. 309-310.

[3] *CO5/862*, no. 30; *CO5/862*, no. 32; *CO5/1312*, no. 21 *et seq.*; *CO5/726*.

[4] Blakiston to the Board of Trade, May 6, 1701; *Board of Trade Journal*, vol. xiv, p. 18; *CO391/14*.

Civil." The province was divided into eleven counties; in each there was a county court consisting of several justices, some counties having more, some less. They each had a commission given them by the governor under the seal of the province and heard and determined such actions as they had cognizance of by their commissions. Belonging to these same courts were the sheriff of the county, a clerk appointed by the crown's secretary in the colony, a cryer and several attorneys. These county courts were held six times in the year in every county, in March, June, August, September, November and January. They determined all petty felonies and misdemeanors arising in their respective counties. A grand jury was usually impaneled three times in the year which might enquire into and receive presentment of all sorts of offenses. If the crime were one which involved the "taking away of life or member", the county court justices could not proceed to trial thereof but had to transmit the proceedings to the provincial court. In civil cases the county courts had power to hold jurisdiction over all actions of debt, contract, replevin, trespass, and battery but in questions of titles of land, freehold or inheritance they had no jurisdiction.[1] The clerk issued the writ in the king's name to the sheriff who arrested the party and the court proceeded to trial. If either party was dissttisfied with the verdict of the jury he might move in arrest of judgment, or if the county court proceeded to judgment on the verdict an appeal might be made to the next provincial court, if the real debt or damage exceeded five pounds sterling or twelve hundred pounds of tobacco. If either party appealed, the appellant was forthwith to produce security and to file the record of the case with the clerk of the provincial court. A writ of error might also be brought from any judgment of a court into the provincial court.

[1] *CO5/726*, p. 65 *et seq.*

The provincial court was held at the seat of government twice in the year. Its jurisdiction extended to all cases arising in the province cognizable by courts of common law. It, therefore, became a court following in the lines of the English Kings' Bench and Common Pleas. From this court appeal might be had to the governor and council; this court was the highest court of common law in Maryland and from it there was appeal only to the King in Council in cases where the value was above three hundred pounds sterling.

Governor Blakiston also listed a court of chancery with a jurisdiction similar to the court of chancery in England extending to all the province.[1] This consisted of a chancellor or keeper of the great seal assisted by one or two of the council, a registrar, a crier and the sheriff of the county and several attorneys attending. A man might have the verdict of this court reversed by the governor and the council if the matter in controversy exceeded fifty pounds sterling or ten thousand pounds of tobacco. An act of the assembly gave the governor and the council this power and created them a superior court of chancery.

There were also two other special courts listed within the province. There was the prerogative or commissary general's court which heard and determined all testamentary affairs, administrations, and legacies; this consisted of one judge, or commissary general and a registrar. Anyone aggrieved by the verdict of this court might appeal to the governor and council. If not satisfied, appeal might be had to the King in Council. The other special court was the court of admiralty consisting of a judge, advocate and registrar appointed under the governor's commission. Its jurisdiction was over all maritime affairs and particularly over cases arising from illegal trading. Here it was indicated again that there was much doubt as to appeals from

[1] *CO5/726*, p. 65 *et seq.*

the court of admiralty, because there seemed to be an inconsistency, the lawyers affirming that appeal from this court should be to the Lord High Admiral, and the king's instructions very plainly stating that all appeals should be to the King in Council.[1]

In December Governor Nicholson of Virginia replied to the circular letter of the Board and enclosed a description of the method of proceeding in the courts of Virginia. He stated plainly that the understanding in Virginia concerning the circular letter was that the English government wished to methodize the colonial courts of justice.[2] He stated that the governor's court, whereof the governor and the council were judges, was the court of law and equity for the hearing and determining of all cases within the dominion of Virginia, except those cases that fell within the jurisdiction of the special court of the admiralty. He was particularly anxious to show that all actions were conducted as nearly as possible according to the common and statute law of England. There were county courts from which appeals were heard. There was jury trial after the accepted English form, the jury being impaneled from the freeholders by the sheriffs of the different counties. The governor's court was appointed to be held on the fifteenth of April and the fifteenth of October of each year. Nicholson's answer did not meet with the entire approval of the Board and in the following March it sent a rather peremptory command for a fuller statement. In July Nicholson again addressed the Board. He gave in detail an account of the establishment and procedure in the admiralty courts within the province.[3]

[1] *CO5/726*, p. 65 *et seq.*

[2] *CO5/1312*, no. 21 et seq. Nicholson to Board of Trade, December 2, 1701.

[3] The letter of the Board of Trade dated March 16, 1702. Nicholson's reply dated July 29, 1702; *CO5/1312*, no. 40.

In New Hampshire Governor William Partridge received his communication from the Board through the Earl of Bellomont who enclosed in a letter the general order asking for a transmission of an account of the methods of proceedings in the several courts. In December of the year 1700, Partridge wrote the Board enclosing a copy of the law of New Hampshire establishing courts of judicature and providing for all trials within the colony. He pointed out that a special regard had been shown to all the directions of the king's commission given him as governor and particularly in all matters relating to appeals. Legal adminstration was in the hands of the justices of the peace, a court of common pleas which had jurisdiction over all matters at common law of not less than twenty pounds value, and a superior court of judicature which met at Portsmouth and whose district was the entire colony. This superior court was the court of last resort in the province to which appeals might regularly come. From this court, an appeal lay to the King in Council in matters exceeding three hundred pounds. An enclosure was made by Partridge of all the oaths used by the justices of the peace and other officials.[1]

From Massachusetts Governor William Stoughton replied to the order in council of July 18, 1700, by sending a complete statement of the methods of proceeding in the Masachusetts courts.[2] All debts, trespass and other matters not exceeding the value of forty shillings, wherein title of land was not concerned were heard, tried and determined by any justice of the peace within his precinct without a jury; these were brought forward either by summons capias or attachment, granted by a justice or the town clerk of the town where the defendant lived, directed to the sheriff of the

[1] William Partridge to the Board of Trade, Dec. 5, 1700; received by the Board and read Feb. 12, 1701; *CO5/862*, no. 30 and enclosures.

[2] *CO5/862*, no. 32, Stoughton to the Board of Trade.

county or his deputies and served and executed at least seven days before the time of trial and hearing.

All civil actions, real and personal, above the value of forty shillings, which might be tried at comon law were originally tried in an inferior court of common pleas held for and within each respective county. This court was constituted for four justices appointed and commissioned by the governor by and with the advice of the council for each county, any three of whom made a quorum. For the whole province there was constituted a superior court of judicature made up of a chief justice and four other justices appointed by the governor, and three of them making a quorum. This court sat in the respective counties at certain places and on certain days assigned by law. In cases where the government was concerned, it lay with the prosecutor to begin his suit either in the inferior courts or in the superior court of judicature at his pleasure. Appeal might be had from the inferior to the superior court and when this was done the executiton was stayed until after the appeal. The whole communication concluded, naively, that the liberty of appeal to the King in Council was provided as was " stated in that behalf in His Majesty's royal charter to the people of Massachusetts ".[1]

That nothing really constructive in the way of an imperial system of judicial administration resulted from this attempt to find out what the colonies would report in the matter is explained not so much by the apathy of the home government as by the events which were crowding upon it. The law officers realized that the officials of the colonial courts were not well trained and that many errors in justice would occur, unless there was a constant watchfulness on the part of the court officials. The Board of Trade and the Privy Council aimed in the eighteenth century to have a fair conformity in

[1] *CO5/862*, no. 32, enclosure ii.

judicial decisions among the different colonies themselves and, so far as England was concerned, a freedom in the matter of appeal with a maintenance by the crown of a review of colonial judicial decisions. There came to be the feeling that with able courts of review there could not be a serious miscarriage of justice without its reaching the attention of some of the crown officials.

Consistent with this policy we find the Board of Trade receiving and reviewing, though with what degree of care can not be judged from the records, the lists of the cases and the proceedings in the various colonial courts.[1] The Board also attempted a scrutiny of various matters with regard to the colonial judiciary. It debated upon the question of the appointment of juries in Virginia and whether the arrangement made by law in that colony was consistent with former practice and not in opposition to English law. It referred the matter finally to the Privy Council.[2] It discussed the question of a want of a chancery court in Massachusetts raised by a memorial of a Mr. Thomas Newton, and ordered that the agent of the colony be sent a copy of the memorial and that he be instructed to obtain the opinion of the attorney and solicitor general thereon.[3] It considered reports from the attorneys general of the different colonies at times very much in detail.[4] The salaries of the attorneys general and other officials were questions which also came before the Board for consideration.[5]

[1] *Board of Trade Journal, CO391/17;* printed volume April, 1704–June, 1705, pp. 10, 35, 83, 87, 196. Records scattered all through the Journals after 1700. *CO5/864,* nos. 118, 119, 121, 122. *CO5/863,* no. 19.

[2] *Board of Trade Journal,* printed vol. 1704-09, p. 385.

[3] *Ibid.,* p. 241.

[4] Report of the Attorney General of Mass. Bay to Governor Belcher concerning the rioters in Frederick's Forts, *CO5/872,* pp. 363-370, Jan. 13, 1700.

[5] *Board of Trade Journal,* printed vol. 1704-09, p. 146, salary of Atwood of New York; that of Bladen of Maryland, p. 182.

It has become evident that the Board of Trade was the clearing house for all suggestions from the governors and complaints which they had to make concerning the legal procedure in their respective colonies. From New York Governor Bellomont wrote in 1700 of the great need for a court of chancery in that province, but added that, since "no body here understands it rightly, I delay appointing one until the Judge and Attorney-General's coming from England." [1] Again, two days later, he urged the Board to send the judge and attorney general, thinking that it would enable him to cope with the assembly.[2] A month later he complained that it was "unhappy that the judge and attorney general are suffered to loiter long in England." [3] Bellomont was probably justified in this impatience as the representation had been drawn by the Board the year before; this lay before the king the necessity of sending an able judge and attorney general to New York.[4] Finally the Bōard secured for New York the appointment of William Atwood as chief justice and Sampson Shelton Broughton as attorney general.

Concerning the famous Allen case in New Hampshire, Bellomont wrote to William Popple, the secretary of the Board, that Colonel Allen had been in Boston to complain to Bellomont about the injustice done him in the superior court of New Hampshire and that a complaint was to be made in England about it. An investigation was to be made and Bellomont took it upon himself to report in order that the Board might be fully informed.[5] Later he wrote that Allen's pretended title to New Hampshire was an impediment to the advantages England might receive from the

[1] Bellomont to Board of Trade, Oct. 17, 1700, *CO5/1045*, no. 1.

[2] Bellomont to Board of Trade, *CO5/1045*, no. 7.

[3] Bellomont to Board of Trade, Nov. 28, 1700, *CO5/1045*, no. 18.

[4] December 11, 1699, *Board of Trade Journal*, vol. iv, p. 291.

[5] Bellomont to William Popple, Boston, March 8, 1700, *CO5/861*.

province.[1] In addition to the Allen case Bellomont reported that an appeal had been refused in Boston to one Lydget by the superior court there in a case concerning which there would no doubt be complaint. He suggested that the lords might investigate why appeals were refused in New England.[2] Over the question of fees in New Hampshire Governor Belcher reported, in answer to the inquiries sent by the home government, that the judges, justices, sheriffs, clerks and all other officers received nothing from the treasury of the colony, but that their fees were fixed by law to be paid by the parties who had been served.[3]

As a result of his correspondence with the Board, Belcher issued a proclamation with regard to officers taking fees, saying that no officers then under his jurisdiction would be permitted to take or receive any other than legal and established fees for their respective services.[4] This question of fees was one which the Board made its special care, feeling that irregularities in this respect had fertile ground in which to develop. The instructions of the governors gave them the power with their councils to regulate fees, but widespread complaint brought the matter before the Board which in turn entered into correspondence with the governors. The colonists were in favor of a regulation of fees by the assemblies of the colonies.

Governor Seymour of Maryland wrote the Board that he would see to the regulation of the judicature according to the directions given him; but he complained of the opposition with which he was contending on the part of the assembly and added that "the provincial court is a mere jest not knowing any rules to guide their judg-

[1] Bellomont to Board of Trade, June 22, 1700, *CO5/861*, no. 45.

[2] Bellomont to Board of Trade, November 28, 1700, *CO5/1045*, no. 18.

[3] *CO5/872*, pp. 425-428.

[4] Proclamation of Governor Belcher, Dec. 3, 1730. *CO5/873*, pp. 15-18.

ments."[1] Two years later he notified the Board of the reduction of the provincial justices to four and the making of necessary provisions to support and enable the four justices to hold their courts and go the circuits thrice yearly. The reduction in number of the provincial justices had created some objection, but the governor was glad to note that the people on the eastern shore had seemed pleased with the new institution.[2]

The Board of Trade, also, had before it the consideration of the chief judicial officials of the colonies. The attorney-general of a colony, though sometimes, was not always appointed by the governor of the colony. As the duty of prosecution lay with this officer his appointment became a matter of some importance. In 1722 this question had become an important issue in the colony of Massachusetts Bay, and the Board made a reference of the question of the appointment of an attorney general for this colony to Robert Raymond, the attorney general of England. He replied by stating that the charters of Massachusetts Bay permitted the appointment of a governor, deputy governor, and secretary only. He further said that the governor with the advice and consent of the council or assistants from time to time could nominate and appoint judges, sheriffs, provost marshal, justices of the peace and other officers belonging to the courts of justice. The general court or assembly had the power to name all civil officers within the provinces. As the office of attorney general was one that fell within the class of judicial officers and since it was the attorney general who attended to and gave his opinion concerning matters of law, his office might properly be said to belong to the council and courts of justice. He was the general law

[1] *CO5/726*, p. 460. Colonel Seymour to Board of Trade, June 10, 1707.

[2] Colonel Seymour to Board of Trade, Dec. 6, 1709. *CO5/727*, p. 146.

officer in suits where the crown was concerned. And therefore it was his opinion that the appointment of the attorney general should belong to the governor by and with the consent of the council or assistants.[1] To the communication forwarded to Massachusetts by the Board, Governor Shute replied that the attorney general's opinion relating to the choosing of a colonial attorney general had been received but that he took the liberty to assure their lordships that the people of Massachusetts paid little or no deference to any opinion or orders that he received from the ministry at home.[2] That the colonists did pay little or no attention to the report was evidenced by the fact that several years later Lieutenant Governor Dummer reported to the Board that in the session of the legislative assembly of 1729 much time had been spent by the representatives over the question of the election of the attorney general which had "been pursued with much heat".[3]

Dudley, in 1705, wrote concerning the irregularities in the province of Rhode Island. He pointed out that subjects of the queen who were not inhabitants of the colony but who sued for debt in the Rhode Island courts could have "no right done them"; that the proceedings in the courts of judicature were very arbitrary and unjust; "that they did not allow of the laws of England to be pleaded in their courts otherwise than it may serve a term for themselves"; that Rhode Island had refused to allow of appeals to the Queen in Council and had given the utmost trouble to those that demanded the same. All these charges he supported

[1] Communication of Robert Raymond, Attorney General, to the Board of Trade, August 10, 1722, in reply to the question of the appointment of the Attorney General for the colony of Mass. Bay made by the Board May 25, 1722. *CO5/868.*

[2] Governor Shute to Board of Trade, Oct. 29, 1722. *CO5/868.*

[3] Dummer to the Board of Trade, Dec. 26, 1729. *CO5/872,* p. 203.

by affidavits setting forth the facts so that the Board might be fully informed concerning the irregularities in the colony.[1] In the same strain Robert Hunter, as governor of New Jersey, wrote that he had displaced all the gentlemen of the council in that colony from being judges and assistants, because matters had become in danger of being determined more by spirit of party than rules of justice, and in order to restore to the people "the benefits of appeal of which they might be bereaved" by the number of assistants on the Board. He also added if a court of chancery should be established in New York one must be established in New Jersey.[2] And Colonel Blakiston reported so small a matter as the substitution of justices of the peace "in room of those dead".[3]

Ordinarily, only civil cases came before the Privy Council, but a single instance will serve as an example to show in what manner the proceedings of a criminal case might reach the crown officials if there was a feeling that injustice had been done. The case of Charles Arabella was brought to the notice of the Board by a petition of one Ann Pauley in 1710. The petition recited that Charles Arabella was indebted to the petitioner who was interested in having justice done and seeing that he was released. Arabella was a native subject of the Duke of Florence, had come to the English colony as a seaman and was at the time the petition had been sent, a prisoner "near Chester River in Maryland at Virginia". He had been charged with blasphemy for which he was tried. He was fined twenty pounds, bored three times through the tongue and sentenced to remain

[1] Dudley to the Board of Trade concerning irregularities in the province of Rhode Island, November 2, 1705. *CO5/1263*, p. 12.

[2] Robert Hunter to the Board of Trade, March 19, 1712. *CO5/1264*, pp. 167-168.

[3] Blakiston to Board of Trade, *CO5/1715*.

six months in prison; all of which punishment the prisoner had undergone with the exception of the payment of the fine which he was unable to raise, and ten pounds additional for the charge of defending himself. Because he could not pay this he had remained over a year in prison.[1] The petition under Lord Dartmouth's signature had been referred by the queen to the Board of Trade in order that it might report what should be done in the matter. The Board considered the report as well as the affidavit of Richard Love, who was the master of the ship in which Arabella had come to Maryland, and on December 8, 1710, reported back to the queen that the fine might be remitted since the prisoner had served the greatest part of the sentence; but the Board further recommended that Arabella be not released until he could be put on board some vessel bound for Europe. The next day December 9, 1710, Lord Dartmouth referred the whole matter back to the Board for reconsideration, feeling that enough thought had not been given the matter. On the twelfth of December the Board again addressed a letter to Dartmouth accompanied among other documents, by a letter from a Mr. John Hyde, who it was stated was a considerable traveller and well informed concerning affairs in the province of Maryland. The Board now recommended clemency.

The most minute details did not escape the attention of the Board through the medium of its correspondence. The lists of cases in the several courts of the different provinces were received and filed.[2] Communication was constantly kept up between the Board of Trade and the colonies con-

[1] Case of Ann Pauley and Charles Arabella, *CO5/727*, pp. 209-212. Petition received November 24, 1710, read November 29th.

[2] *CO5/863*, no. 19; *CO5/864*, nos. 118, 119, 121, 122; for the months of September and October in New York, *Board of Trade Journal*, printed volume, 1704-1709, pp. 9, 87, 196.

cerning judicial affairs. These were, for example, letters to the home government from Maryland in obedience to instructions from the attorney general concerning the laws of Maryland for a period of years.[1] The attorney general of New York reported his opinion relating to wines imported from the Madeira Islands by one Captain Davison.[2] Lists of fines and forfeitures imposed by colonal courts were regularly received.[3] The Board of Trade recommended appointments to colonial positions in recommendation of the Bishop of London.[4]

By a review of the legislation passed by the various colonial assemblies the home government kept a diligent watch upon all laws tending to encroach upon individual right or the imperial prerogative, and by use of the veto upon such legislation kept the colonies from departing from established English custom.[5] The English government wished that the rules and the procedure in the colonial courts should correspond as much as possible to the methods used in Great Britain.

The president and council together with the general assembly of Maryland sent an address to the home government concerning irregularity in judicial procedure. This address stated that the governor of Maryland, who was also chancellor, sat as the judge of his own decree when there was an appeal from a judgment in chancery. This practice

[1] 1692-1694, 1695-1697, 1698. *CO5/714*, p. 75.

[2] *Board of Trade Journal*, March 29, 1704; printed volume, 1704-1709, p. 87.

[3] *Ibid.*, p. 83.

[4] *Ibid.*, p. 57.

[5] This subject has been very adequately discussed in *Columbia University Studies in History, Economics and Public Law*, vol. lxiv, no. 2, Russell, E. B., *Review of American Colonial Legislation by the King in Council.* With regard to the legislation concerning judicial affairs, see particularly chapter v, pp. 161-168.

it was contended was repugnant to English rules and methods of justice. The answer of the home government was an order in council disallowing the Maryland act entitled, "An Act for Appeals and regulating Writs of Error". This act revised and reenacted a previous act dealing with the same subject. The Board of Trade had particularly recommended the dissallowance of this law, on the ground that appeals in Maryland should be brought from the inferior courts to the governor and council and thence to the Privy Council in accordance with the instructions to the governor. The effect of this would be to render Maryland practice the same as that in the other plantations.[1]

It was not an uncommon thing for the colonists to petition for redress of grievances by requesting the home government to use its authority and disallow law when the courts of justice had failed to give relief. Through John Montague of Chancery Lane several hundred owners of land and principal inhabitants of the province of New York petitioned the home government in 1700, for the disallowance of a law with regard to taxation. The act was to be considered on the ground that it did personal injustice. Ebenezer Wilson and Samuel Burt, farmers of the excise of "the island of Naragansett", had refused to render an account of what they had farmed from the respective towns, counties and manors for the year. The men had lost by their farming of the excise and were unwilling to make public such a loss lest it should prejudice their credit. The governor sent for them and extra-judicially required them to give an account upon oath which they refused to do. This oath was likewise administered to them extra-judicially by the governor. Upon recommendation of the governor

[1] Act of October, 1704, revising and re-enacting Act of July, 1699. Reported by Board of Trade and disallowed by order in council, June 14, 1711. *CO5/717*.

the legislative body passed an act committing the men for refusal. This act was declared by the petition to be *ex post facto* and the colonial government condemned as guilty of arbitrary proceeding along with a violation of the requirements of English law. The act was denounced as made to countenance or excuse an illegal act of the governor and for that reason it was stated that it should be repealed.[1]

The Bayard case in New York brought a petition from Henry Adderby and Charles Lodwick, merchants, which the Council referred to the attorney and solicitor general. The memorial recited that Colonel Nicholas Bayard of New York had been indicated and convicted and had had sentence of death and forfeiture passed upon him because of an act of the assembly which made it high treason in any way to disturb the peace of the government. The petition asked that Bayard be allowed to bring a writ of error, requesting that the judgment of the colonial court be reversed and that for that purpose the record and the minutes of all the evidence at the trial should be sent to England for review.[2] The attorney and solicitor general reported July 2, 1702, that the proceedings against Colonel Bayard were very extraordinary and recommended that he be permitted to appeal from a conviction of treason in New York and that he be admitted to bail on the giving of sufficient security. The act under which he had been condemned, all the records in the case and the minutes of the evidence taken, were to be transmitted to the Board. This act had declared that any person who should by any manner or upon any pretense whatsoever by force of arms or otherwise disturb the peace, good and quiet of the government of their late Majesties King William and Mary as it was then established, should

[1] *CO5/1044*, pp. 309-331. Memorial of John Montague of Chancery Lane London to Board of Trade. Received August 13, 1700.

[2] *Acts Privy Council, Colonial Series*, vol. ii, no. 875, pp. 412-413.

be "deemed as rebels and traitors unto their Majesties and incur the pains, penalties and forfeitures as the law of England had provided for such offenses." [1] On a report of the committee of the whole council, July 9, 1702, Lord Cornbury was directed to induce the assembly of New York to repeal this act defining high treason because the meaning had been misinterpreted.[2] On the same day Broughton was restored to his office of attorney general of New York from which he had been suspended by the lieutenant governor and council on account of his opinion on the charge against Colonel Bayard.

The home government attempted to watch by this method of review any encroachment of the legislatures upon the ordinary judicial functions in the colonies. An act passed in New Hampshire enabling certain citizens, Daniel Merrill, John Hale and Henry Hale Jr., to review and prosecute, in the course of law, actions wherein they were defendants and in which they claimed they had been defaulted, was disallowed August 12, 1768, because the matter was not of such nature as to be the concern of the legislature but was cognizable in the courts of law. It was stated that the parties could have by trial what they were denied and consequently this act offered to the colonial government an opportunity to restrain and direct the proceedings in courts of law, which was considered highly improper.[3]

Nor would the English government permit the legislatures of the province to move the courts from one place to another to the detriment of judicial procedure. An act of the New Hampshire legislative assembly dated December 3, 1730, was referred to the committee by the King in Council in 1735. This act had provided for the removal of three

[1] *Acts Privy Council, Colonial Series,* vol. ii, no. 875, pp. 412-413.

[2] *Ibid.*

[3] *Acts Privy Council,* vol. v, no. 82, pp. 160-161.

of the courts of general quarter sessions and an inferior court of common pleas from Portsmouth to Exeter, Hampton and Dover. The Board of Trade recommended its disallowance. On March 7, 1735, the committee agreed with the Board of Trade that the act should be repealed, not only because there seemed no reason for removing the above mentioned courts from Portsmouth which was the capital of New Hampshire and much more populous than any other town in that province, but also because of "the great number of saw mills erected at Exeter, Hampton and Dover which might give great encouragement to the distruction of Your Majesty's woods because these towns being the chief seats of the loggers or wood cutters it would be very difficult if not impracticable to find a jury there who would given an impartial verdict between Your Majesty and the Offenders." [1]

Legislation was disallowed which seemed to violate time-honored English custom with regard to juries, habeas corpus, or the taking of oaths in colonial courts. A Virginia law concerning juries was the subject of consideration by the Board of Trade in 1707, but when it was determined that it was according to former practice and not in opposition to English law it was referred to the queen for approval.[2] A South Carolina Act confirming and establishing the ancient and approved method of drawing jurors by ballot in that province, for the appointing of special courts for the trial of causes of transient persons, and giving power to the provost marshal to allow the proof of deeds beyond the seas as evidence, was referred by the Privy Council to its committee, together with a Board of Trade representation for its disallowance.[3] The act was repealed on November 31,

[1] *Acts Privy Council,* vol. iii, no. 328, pp. 453-454.

[2] *Board of Trade Journal,* printed volume, 1704-1709, p. 385.

[3] *Acts Privy Council,* vol. iii, p. 448.

1738. In 1733 certain South Carolina citizens, Thomas Cooper, James Greene and Rowland Vaughan, complained of the proceedings of the assembly in their province, and among other things of an act passed entitled "An Act for the Prevention of Suits and Disturbances to His Majesty's Judges and Magistrates on account of the Habeas Corpus Act." The petition was referred to the Board of Trade in December 1733, and in April of the next year the committee of the Privy Council heard counsel on the Board of Trade report. The committee reported that the act was of an extraordinary character and that there was no clause inserted for suspending the execution until the royal pleasure should be known; it was also contrary to the twenty-fourth article of the instructions of the king to the governor and so ought to be replaced. This was ordered some few days later.[1]

The officials of the crown watched colonial legislation carefully for the purpose of detecting irregular judicial enactments. Jackson, the special attorney for the king, reported the disallowance of a New York law which empowered justices of the peace, mayors, recorders and aldermen to try causes to the value of ten pounds, saying that it was by no means proper in point of law, inasmuch as it ran directly contrary to the judicial policy of the home government; it could not "but occasion mischievous effects under the specious appearance of facilitating justice".[2] Mr. Jackson also reported the disallowance of a New York law in 1774 because it provided for purgation by oath in a criminal matter; this, it was stated, was contrary to the genius of laws in England and could not but prove too frequently an irresistible temptation to perjury.[3] A Massa-

[1] *Acts Privy Council*, no. 286, p. 396.

[2] *Acts Privy Council*, vol v, no. 168, pp. 284-285.

[3] *Ibid.*, no. 299, p. 399.

chusetts act which provided for three trials in the courts of that province before a sentence or judgment in any case could be final or conclusive, and between each of those trials allowing an interval of three years to elapse, was disallowed in 1700 as delaying justice unnecessarily and being vexatious.[1] Likewise the home government forbade in all cases where the question with regard to legislation arose, the use of affidavits as evidence in courts and the serving of writs contrary to the practice of England.[2]

The fifth method of control was decision by the King in Council in cases brought upon appeal. These decisions were of two kinds: first, those in which there was an attempt made to control court procedure and judicial administration in the colonies, and second, those in which the facts in the case had been reviewed and the judgment of the colonial courts upheld or reversed on the basis of these facts. It was not an uncommon thing for the home government to order a case dismissed or the commencement of a new trial. These two classes of decisions as methods of imperial control will be discussed in subsequent chapters, but it should be particularly noted that the first was the common method of correcting colonial court procedure and attempting to mould it to the accepted English standard.

Thus it may be seen that by the five methods above enumerated the English government attempted to know and direct the main lines of development of the judicial system of the provinces. The home government felt rightly that unless there was some agency to oversee and admonish the colonial officials the provinces would not conform to any one judicial pattern. Unless the provinces did conform to such a pattern and appeals were encouraged, it was felt that justice

[1] *CO5/909*, pp. 248, 249.

[2] *Vide* Russell, *Review of American Colonial Legislation*, p. 163.

would be left in the hands of incompetent courts. The great distance from England, the lack of expert legal advisers in the colonies and the general apathy of the colonies to an imperial program rendered the work of the home government extremely difficult.

CHAPTER II

THE KING IN COUNCIL

IT is evident from what has been said that the controlling factor in the imperial management of the colonial judicial system was the King in Council. It was the fountain of justice, the source for the determination of all matters of judicial importance. Through its various committees as well as through the imperial agencies at its disposal it could reach any phase of colonial life. Its power with regard to the examination of legal questions was in theory limitless. In its administrative capacity it could control the execution and procedure of colonial courts and all other matters in the administration of justice. As a court of review it possessed the power of passing upon cases which had been in the colonial courts. It was the center from which radiated the administration of justice.

The affairs of the dependencies had always received attention and consideration from the governmental agencies in England. As early as the reign of Edward I we hear of "receivers and triers of Petitions" whose duty it was to hear complaints from Ireland and the island of Guernsey.[1] In the early Tudor period the custom became definitely fixed that appeals from these possessions should be heard

[1] *Rotuli Parliamentorum*, vol. i, p. 159; vol. xxiii Edward I, pp. 159-187, "et aussi assigna le Roi sire Johan de Berewyk, sire Hervey de Stanton, William de Dene, William de Mortimer and Roger de Beanson, de receiure toutes les peticions de ceux de Ireland et de Ile de Gernessye et de respondre a celles toutes."

by the King in Council.[1] This became the established practice in the late Tudor and the whole of the Stuart periods.

The methods by which appeals reached the home government was regulated by a series of orders in council. These gave the general and basic ruling which was to form the method of appeal. It was not until the late seventeenth century that an order in council touched the regulation of appeals from the American colonies.

The first definite statement which we have concerning the Privy Council as a court of appellate jurisdiction for foreign possessions is found in 1572 for the Isle of Jersey.[2] In this order in council the following principles were laid down: first, no appeal was to be admitted or allowed from any sentence or judgment in any matter or cause not exceeding the value of seven pounds sterling of current English money; second, no appeal in any cause or matter, great or small was to be permitted or allowed before it should be fully examined and ended by definitive sentence or other judgment having the same force and effect; third, that every appeal was to be prosecuted within three months next ensuing "except there be just cause of lett or impediment to be proved before their Lordships being the Judges of Appeals and by their Lordships allowed"; fourth, no appeal was to be allowed without a copy of the sentence or judgment and the "whole process of the cause closed" together under the seal of the Isle and this copy furnished within eight days after the request was made for it. These statements were made more definite later by the order in council of May 19, 1671:

[1] An order in council of Henry VII (1495) ordered that henceforth no appeal from the islands should be to any court in England but only 'au Roi et Conseil".

[2] *Acts Privy Council*, 1571-1575, vol. viii, pp. 75-76.

that no appeal for moveable goods or personal estate henceforth be allowed unless it be of the value of three hundred livres tournois per annum; nor for inheritance or other real estate unless of the value of five hundred livres tournois per annum.[1]

It may be seen that even thus early general principles were established for the appeal of cases to the Privy Council for districts lying outside the realm. There must be a definite sum involved. A decision must have been made from which an appeal was taken. A time limit must be set in which the case might be appealed. All the facts of the case and the whole process in the inferior courts must be presented. The importance of the general principles here stated lies in the fact that they became the precedents for the imperial control of the administration of justice through the agency of appeals to the King in Council; although they undergo modification in the seventeenth and eighteenth centuries we are still able to distinguish the general basic outlines of these precedents in the rules laid down for the American colonies.

With the establishment of the American colonies by Englishmen the idea of appeal for redress of grievances to the King in Council seems to have been assumed although in the early period there are not many evidences of its use.[2] The appeal might be in this early period a judicial appeal from a case tried in the colonial courts or it might be any sort of an appeal from the colonies. Every kind of an appeal was recognized by the Council.

The first regulation which we have concerning colonial

[1] *P. C. 2*, no. 63, p. 15, no. 13. Rules and Orders to be observed in ye Court of Jersey. Whitehall, May 19, 1671.

[2] In 1683, in the case of Jennett *vs.* Bishop, Lord Keeper North affirmed the principle that an appeal lay to the sovereign in council from places held under grant from the crown.

appeals is in 1684. One Robert Wadleigh petitioned from New Hampshire stating that he had come "at great trouble and charge from Great Island" for the hearing of an appeal the order of which had been served upon him in March. Upon examination it was found that security had not been given and January 23, 1684, the order in council was issued that "no appeals to the Board from the Plantation be admitted for the future unless security be given by the appellants to prosecute their appeals effectually and accept the King's award".[1]

The appeal to the King in Council was the means of prime importance used in the regulation and control of the administration of justice by the imperial government. The litigant who was dissatisfied with the decision of the colonial court might petition for a hearing before the King in Council. If this were denied by the colonial court for any reason he might then petition the Privy Council in a direct manner that his appeal be admitted and heard. The Privy Council generally referred this to "the Lords of the Committee for hearing appeals from the Plantations" or as it is better known the Committee for Appeals.[2]

This committee referred to as "the committee" seems to have been a standing one. It is variously referred to in the documents, but it was a general body to which all matters of colonial interest were sent. The word committee does not seem to imply the attendance of any particular persons, but this group usually consisted of the Bishop of London, a secretary of state and such others as would interest themselves in the matter. Until 1696 this committee was an indefinite one appointed by the Privy Council itself but in that year it was ordered:

[1] *Acts Privy Council, Colonial Series,* vol. ii, p. 53, no. 123; *Calendar State Papers,* vol. vi, no. 1518.

[2] *Acts Privy Council,* vol. ii, no. 657, p. 310.

That all appeals from any of the Plantations be heard as formerly by a Committee who are to report the matters so heard by them with their opinion thereupon to His Majesty in Council. And in order thereunto His Majesty did declare his further pleasure, that all the Lords of the Council or any three or more of them, be appointed a committee for that purpose.[1]

Later, July 5, 1727, this order was reaffirmed and again in 1761.[2] The committee, therefore, passed upon the right of an individual to appeal, reviewed the facts of the case which had been appealed and reported back to the King in Council who gave a final decision on the matter.

The regular mode of dealing with colonial affairs from 1675 till May 1696 was to refer the matter in hand for consideration to a committee of the Privy Council known as the "Lords of the Committee of Trade and Plantations" and to issue an order in council more or less in accordance with the report made by this body. In May, 1696, this committee gave way to the "Lords Commissioners of Trade and Plantations" or, as it is more generally known, the Board of Trade. This transition is markedly brought out in a case appealed by Richard Holder and Wylde Clarke, merchants of London, against the condemnation at Bardados of their ship *Experiment*. The appeal is referred to "the Rt. Honorable the Lords of the Committee of Trade and Plantations to examine the matter of the said petition and to report to the Board what they do conceive fit for His Majesty to do therein".[3] Upon the reading of the report of the Committee of Trade and Plantations, the Council admitted the appeal and appointed a day for the

[1] *Acts Privy Council*, vol. ii, no. 657.

[2] *Acts Privy Council*, vol. iii, no. 124; *ibid.*, vol. iv, no. 448.

[3] *P. C. 2*, no. 76, p. 92.

hearing.[1] Upon the day named Holder and Clarke set forth that they were ready to be heard upon their appeal and it was then ordered that the whole matter be referred to "the Council of Trade to examine the business by hearing the parties concerned." [2] But when the case was finally settled January 21, 1697, by a reversal of judgment given at Barbadoes in November 1693, it was plainly stated that the King in Council was acting on a report from "the Lords of the Committee of the whole Council".[3] In a word, the case had been referred to the old Committee of Trade and Plantations, then to the Board of Trade, but it was the newly created committee for appeals instituted the previous December that reported the case January 1697.

After the creation of the Board of Trade, the spheres of the Board and the committee for appeals tended to overlap and encroach one upon the other. The outcome of this was to enlarge the scope of duties and widen the functions of the committee. Thus when one Henry Peers of Barbados petitioned that a law passed in that province might be repealed and all proceedings under this legislation be stayed, the matter was referred to the committee for appeals.[4] The committee for appeals reported April 15, 1713, recommending the removal of certain persons named by Governor Hunter of New Jersey as unfit to sit in the council of New Jersey.[5] Also, there were considered by the committee a representation from the Board of Trade June 25, 1719, for removing Mr. Byrd from the council of Virginia because of continued absence from the colony and recommending Peter Beverly as his successor, together with

[1] *Acts Privy Council*, vol. iii, p. 241.

[2] *P. C. 2*, no. 76, p. 532.

[3] *Ibid.*, p. 573.

[4] *Acts Privy Council*, vol. ii, no. 1333.

[5] *CO5/995*, p. 302.

Mr. Byrd's petition of protest against this. The decision of the committee for appeals was that Byrd should be continued, since he had engaged to return with the first ship to Virginia and that his stay in England had been due to accidental causes.[1] Both the Board of Trade and the committee for appeals heard the complaints against Colonel Daniel Park governor of the Leeward Islands.[2] The petition of Sir Charles Cox that the governor of Barbados be restrained from suspending Cox's brother from the council of that colony was also heard by both bodies.[3] The council referred petitions to the Board of Trade at times exactly as if the Board had the appellate jurisdiction belonging to the committee for appeals.[4] In one instance the appeal of a petitioner was admitted on recommendation of the Board of Trade.[5]

The administration of justice in the colonies was the constant care of the Privy Council. When an appeal was admitted the colonial court was directed to send over sealed copies of all the proceedings. Thus copies of the proceedings were ordered sent from New York under seal of the province in the case of Alsop *v.* Vandall.[6] Also, the court of Boston in Massachusetts Bay was ordered to certify the record of all proceedings in the case of Samuel Allen appealing from the judgment of the superior court of Boston.[7] Rhode Island courts were ordered to perfect their records and transmit them with an account of their method of pro-

[1] *Acts Privy Council,* vol. ii, no. 1321.

[2] *Ibid.,* no. 1083, pp. 597-8.

[3] *Ibid.,* no. 1329; *Board of Trade Journal,* 1704-1709, p. 413.

[4] *Acts Privy Council,* vol. ii, nos. 843, 844.

[5] *Ibid.,* no. 845.

[6] *Ibid.,* no. 800.

[7] *Acts Privy Council,* vol. ii, no. 972.

cedure and a statement as to whether the cases in the records produced before the Privy Council were complete accounts of the proceedings on both sides.[1] On January 3, 1704, the committee recommended that the court of assistants in Connecticut send over copies of all proceedings and give reason why Edward Palmes had been refused the right of appeal from two sentences of the provincial court and that, upon giving the proper security, all parties concerned in both cases should attend to be heard on the first council day in October 1704.[2]

When the proceedings had been duly transmitted the appellant petitioned the Council for "a short day" for hearing his appeal. This petition was referred to the committee for appeals, who fixed a day for examining the case. The case was heard before the committee, counsel for both sides being admitted to plead. In the eighteenth century the case was generally very well prepared before the date set for the hearing and printed copies of the pleas of both sides were made.[3] After the case had been heard before the committee a report was made and presented to the Council. Almost invariably an order was issued by the Council within a short time carrying out the suggestions made by the committee upon the hearing of the case. The order in council issued upon this recommendation might affirm decisions of the colonial courts, reverse the previous decisions or alter them. An appeal was sometimes dismissed with eighty, forty, thirty, twenty, ten or five pound ster-

[1] *Acts Privy Council*, vol. ii, no. 1301.

[2] *Ibid.*, no. 913; All documents *CO5/1263*, pt. ii, p. 72.

[3] See Hardwicke Papers. *British Museum Additional MSS.*, nos. 36216-36220. These are briefs as presented by the solicitors to the committee. They are in printed form as prepared for the hearing of the case and the notes largely in the handwriting of Charles Yorke show the care with which the various legal arguments were prepared.

ling costs.[1] Or the case might be dismissed for non-prosecution.[2]

Sometimes a case was dismissed because it had not come to the Council in a regular manner. Thus John Oulton and Cornelius Waldo of Boston petitioned in 1717 for permission to appeal from a judgment of the superior court of Suffolk County, Massachusetts Bay, in favor of Arthur Savage, master of the *Province,* a galley, in a suit commenced by the petitioners. On February 18, 1718, when the committee considered the case they reported that they were in favor of dismissing the appeal as the petitioners had not applied for a review in New England as it was still possible for them to do.[3]

At times a case was dismissed at the instance of the attorney for the parties. Alexander Grant of Newport, Rhode Island, brought an appeal to the King in Council in 1769 from the colonial courts in which he had been condemned to pay 251 pounds sterling and costs for the value of certain bills of exchange. In 1771 the appeal was dismissed on the information of the solicitor in the case that he had no orders to proceed further.[4]

By the eighteenth century definite rules following the earlier precedents were laid down concerning appeals from the American colonies. The usual conditions for appeals were that the appeal must be granted by the court giving the decision, usually within fourteen days after judgment had been rendered. The appeal should be entered within the period of a year and a day, though this does not seem to have been imperative. The value of the matter in dis-

[1] *Acts Privy Council,* vol. iv, nos. 145, 223; vol. iii, nos. 409, 451, 455; vol. ii, no. 770.

[2] *Acts Privy Council,* vol. iii, nos. 362, 365, 442.

[3] *Acts Privy Council,* vol. ii, no. 1270, p. 721.

[4] *Acts Privy Council,* vol. v, no. 125.

pute must be of a certain amount. This varied from some 200 pounds to 500 pounds in the different colonies. Generally speaking, it was expected that the sum involved would be of at least 300 pounds sterling. Security had to be given by the appellant for costs; also he had to give enough security to show that he would prosecute the case and that he would be responsible if the Council determined against him.[1] The execution of the judgment of the colonial court was not to be suspended unless ample security were made to cover possible damages. The only exceptions to these rules were that all cases involving a question of customs duties or illegal trading might be appealed without any of these restrictions. Also, cases in which the clergy were involved might be taken on appeal directly.[2]

When the case did not involve the requisite amount a petition could be made directly to the Council, which, if it wished, could admit the appeal. Cases were frequently dismissed on the recommendation of the committee when it was found that the sum involved was under value. In 1773 Robert Keeler, one time captain of the ship *Mercury*, petitioned to be admitted to an appeal from the judgment of the superior court of Rhode Island in March of that year in an action of assault commenced by William Rhodes against him, although the sum of 94 pounds recovered by Rhodes was less than the law required in cases of appeal. In December the committee reported back that it did not think it necessary to comply with the prayer of the petition when the amount was under value.[3]

[1] See Chalmers, *Opinions*, vol. ii, p. 177.

[2] *Acts Privy Council*, vol. ii, pp. 237-241. Upon a question of appeal raised by Jahleel Brenton, a custom official, the Council established the precedent of admitting customs appeals. The case is discussed later, *infra*, chapter iii.

[3] *Acts Privy Council*, vol. v, no. 272, p. 384. *Vide* also *infra*, chapter iii, as well as the appeal of John Taylor of London, merchant, 1707. *Acts Privy Council*, vol. ii, no. 1019.

In another case involving the questions of time limit and jurisdiction the attitude of the Council may be noted. Samuel Pike, a merchant of London, brought suit in the Pennsylvania courts over a question of the estate of his brother, Richard Pike. The estate was located in Pennsylvania. The Supreme Court of Pennsylvania, rejecting what seemed to Pike very material evidence, gave judgment against him, March 20, 1760. Pike's counsel took exception to the verdict in order to appeal to the King in Council. He asked through his attorney that in as much as he had not received the record of the case from the court at Philadelphia he might be permitted to prosecute his appeal even after the expiration of the time limit in Pennsylvania. The petition was referred to the committee in September, 1770 and in December of that year the committee ordered that the appeal be not admitted unless all documents should be presented on or before February 12, 1771. In June the appeal was dismissed with twenty pounds sterling costs for non-prosecution.[1]

The instructions by which the governors of the colonies were restrained from admitting appeals to the King in Council except in cases where the sum or matter in dispute was of a certain amount were considered as restraints upon the colonial officials alone and did not by any means preclude the King in Council from entertaining appeals in cases of any value where it was thought fit to do so.[2] Petition might also be made direct to the king for special leave to appeal if the case did not meet the usual conditions. This was generally granted in civil cases of substantial importance from a constitutional or legal point of view. With regard to criminal cases, the King in Council would not review or interfere with the course of criminal proceedings in any

[1] *Acts Privy Council,* vol. v, no. 161, pp. 280-281.

[2] Chalmers, *Opinions,* vol. ii, pp. 177-178.

colonial court unless it was shown that by a disregard of the principles of natural justice or otherwise grave injustice had been done.[1]

The rule that the execution of colonial judgments should not be suspended received consideration in 1726, and as a result was amended by order in council. On July fifth the matter was under discussion and it was represented that in the instructions to the governors there was proviso that execution was not to be suspended by reason of an appeal to the King in Council in case a judgment first given by an inferior court had been confirmed by the governor and council. By means of this proviso executions had been immediately issued notwithstanding the fact that an appeal had been requested and was depending before the Council. In defense of this practice it was shown that great inconveniences had arisen where the appellee had become insolvent or had withdrawn himself and his effects from the province before the decision of the Council could be known and had so left the appellant without any redress. Additional instructions were ordered to be prepared for the governors requiring them, notwithstanding the proviso to suspend the execution of any judgment or decree which was appealed until the same should have been determined in England, unless the appellee gave good and sufficient security for ample restitution to the appellant.[2]

The Council was anxious that in its determination of cases coming before it on appeal the legislation of the different provinces might be understood and acted upon in the final decision. In 1752 the Council directed the Board of Trade to prepare instructions to the governors in order that this might be accomplished:

Whereas some of the proprietary and charter governments in

[1] Chalmers, *Opinions*, vol. ii, pp. 177-178.

[2] *Acts Privy Council*, vol. iii, no. 100, pp. 126-127.

America though empowered to make laws are not required to transmit such laws to His Majesty for his approbation or disallowance yet in regard appeals are frequently brought before His Majesty in Council from the judgments and decrees made in the several courts of judicature within the said governments the determination whereof depends upon being duly informed of the laws subsisting there, it is therefore thought expedient that these respective governments should transmit hither as soon as conveniently may be a true and authentic copy of all their laws now in force.[1]

It is not surprising that delays occurred and that there should have been attempts to regulate the procedure. On January 18, 1728, the Council ordered that when a day had been appointed to hear any appeals or complaints either from the Plantations or the Isles of Jersey and Guernsey or for any other matter coming before the committee that want of counsel would be no reason for deferring the hearing.[2] And again in March 1731, the lords of the committee tried to correct the procedure by stating that documents and papers setting forth the facts in the cases had been presented to the committee without any signature of counsel or any observance of the niceties of legal practice. Two days later, March 10, 1731, the Council ordered that henceforth the committee would not receive any printed matter unless the same were signed by one or more of the counsel who should attend a hearing of the case.[3] Again, April 21, 1746, it was necessary to state that when a day of hearing had been

[1] *Acts Privy Council*, vol. iv, no. 167, p. 153. It is interesting to note in this connection that when the instruction in accordance with the representation of 1752 reached Massachusetts the Lieutenant Governor reported April 19. 1753, that "the Assembly have not thought proper to take any notice thereof, being very tenacious of the present laws and adverse to any alterations." *Ibid.*, p. 207.

[2] *Acts Privy Council*, vol. iii, p. 182.

[3] *Acts Privy Council*, vol. iii, p. 310.

set, the party or parties at whose request such appeal or cause had been set down should be in readiness to be heard and that the cases, having been put on the list of business for hearing, would be heard in the course in which they were set down without further notice or direction.[1] In order to have a complete understanding upon the matter certain days were decreed as standing days for the hearing of cases from the plantations. These were the day before the first seal (appointed by the lord chancellor) preceding every term at ten o'clock in the morning and upon the day of the second seal preceding Michaelmas, Hilary and the Easter terms.[2] No cases were to be heard on any of the days above mentioned except those that had been duly set down and due notice was to be given to the parties on or before the sittings of the committee. The printed documents were to be delivered by the appellants or their agents or solicitors to the council office at least one week before the day on which the appeal was to be heard. Neglect of either party to comply with these instructions would not delay the hearing of the appeal provided one party had delivered the papers and applied to the Council for a hearing.[3]

The procedure followed in hearing appeals present some interesting details. Summons were issued by the Council for parties concerned in the appeals. Captain William Dyer appealed to be released from the charge of high treason brought against him in 1681 in New York by one Samuel Winder. The committee recommended that the king "direct an advertisement to be put in the Gazett" that Winder appear within one month; this was also to be published on the Royal Exchange as well as sent to the mayor of South-

[1] *Acts Privy Council,* vol. iv, p. 15.

[2] *Acts Privy Council,* vol. v, p. 397.

[3] *Ibid.*, p. 398.

ampton where it was thought Winder was located.[1] At another time in the revival of an appeal in the name of Hannah, wife of Godfrey Laycock, from Rhode Island in 1767 a summons was affixed on the Royal Exchange and in the New England Coffee House.[2] Cases were sometimes heard *ex parte,* generally on demand from the solicitors of the appellant when the other parties failed to make an appearance. The list of appeals fails to show that this was done frequently or that there was any injustice attached to it. When the appeals were heard before the committee it became a court at law, heard solicitors for both parties and possessed the right to examine witnesses or refer matters to the other imperial agencies. Its decision was the report to the Council. The greatest number of appeals came from the New England colonies of Rhode Island and Massachusetts and from Virginia and New York. Maryland and Pennsylvania were represented by a smaller number. There was a scattering number through the other colonies, with the exception of Georgia from which there were but two appeals and one complaint to the Council. These two appeals concerned shipping and interrupted voyages; the complaint was against the magistrates and the trustees of the province for the imprisonment of a resident for more than two years.[3]

Unlike appeals from the East Indies and Canada which involved Hindoo, Mohammedan and French law, the appeals from the American colonies depended upon English law as modified by local acts and regulations. The Council showed the greatest desire to become acquainted with the

[1] *Acts Privy Council,* vol. ii, no. 47, p. 24.

[2] Laycock *v.* Clarke and Southwicke, *Acts Privy Council,* vol. v, no. 46, p. 115.

[3] *Acts Privy Council,* vol. iii, no. 402, pp. 562-563; vol. iv, no. 150; *ibid.*, no. 265.

local law and to judge impartially by its standards where they did not conflict with accepted English tradition. In cases involving the merchant class it was not unusual to submit the proposition involved to a committe selected by both parties for arbitration.[1] This committee was usually made up of merchants resident in London to whom the question of accounts could be submitted. In every respect great care was taken that the case coming on appeal should be decided in a satisfactory manner. The most eminent judges and lawyers were often present and concurred in the decree. At a hearing of a case in 1726 the Lords Chief Justices Raymond and Eyre, Sir Joseph Jekyll, Master of Rolls and Lords Trevor attended.[2] But the fact to be regretted was that an appeal to the King in Council could be undertaken only by those with considerable means, since an appeal was by far the most expensive legal procedure then known.

In 1696, though the appellate jurisdiction of the Privy Council was still retained, the center of the English colonial administration was shifted to the Board of Trade or as it was called the "Lords of Trade and Plantations" or more simply the Lords of Trade.[3] By the commission through which it was created the Board of Trade was made the official committee to which complaints and memorials for redress of grievances were to be directed and was to report to the King in Council concerning the proper determination in all cases referred to it. It also had authority to send for persons, examine affidavits and papers and hear witnesses on oath.[4] The Board could draw upon the afficials of the crown for advice and direction. In this connection it

[1] *Acts Privy Council*, vol. iii, no. 65; *ibid.*, no. 321.

[2] Cooper, *Parliamentary Procedure*, pp. 224-225.

[3] *Board of Trade Journal*, vol. ix. *N. Y. Colonial Documents*, vol. iv, p. 145.

[4] *N. Y. Colonial Documents*, vol. iv, p. 148.

made use of the services of the attorney general and solicitor general for advice in the matter of legal technicalities. It addressed communications to the Bishop of London, the lords of treasury, the postmaster general and the lords of the admiralty. It felt free to call before it persons informed as to affairs in the colonies and asked information of persons who were in a position to know the facts in any given case. Executive or administrative orders were not issued by the Board on its own authority but the findings in a given case were embodied in a report or representation to the King in Council or to "the committee" and this final decision was recorded as an order in council.

As was shown earlier at the time that the Board of Trade was created, the judicial affairs of the Channel Islands and the colonies were assigned by the Council to committees which conducted an investigation and reported back to the Council. This arrangement was not destroyed in the matter of appeals by the creation of the Board of Trade. The appeal was made directly to the King in Council, and the Board of Trade, being called upon by a reference of the case to it, gathered facts, reviewed the situation and made a representation to the Council. The committee for appeals then acted as a court where both parties could be heard, the hearing being conducted as if an appeal had been made from the findings of the Board before it. The committee recommended final action to the Council and this was embodied in the final order in council.

Definite examples will show the working of the system. When Francis Brinley petitioned the Council in 1699 complaining of obstruction of appeals from Rhode Island the petition was referred to the Board of Trade. The Board wrote Mr. Samuel Cranston concerning the matter and ordered the Earl of Bellomont to make inquiry into such irregularity as he might find. The Board conducted an examination and made a representation to the Council concerning the general question of appeals, and the order in council concerning the inherent right of the Crown to hear appeals was the result.[1] Upon an order of the Council the Board took up the question of appeals in Connecticut in the famous Palmes case. After communicating with Mr. Wharton, the solicitor for the governor and company of Connecticut, the Board made a representation to the Council stating that after consultation with the attorney and solicitor general the Board was of the opinion that an appeal should be admitted.[2] When the question of the execution of martial law upon soldiers in pay in the colonial service came up the Board drew up the instructions to the governors in accordance with an order in council. The several drafts were transmitted in a letter to Mr. Vernon as secretary that they might be presented to the King and receive his approval.[3] The case of Winthrop *v.* Lechmere from Connecticut shows the workings of the system in such a way that if the appeal involved a purely judicial question it was settled by the committee and not referred to the Board. But if the appeal involved a question administrative in character it was regularly referred to the Board for consideration.[4]

The Board passed through several various phases of activity. During the early years of its existence its meetings were frequent and its decisions prompt. Its efficiency declined in the early years of the eighteenth century and with the accession of George I in 1714 and under Walpole

[1] *Co391/12*, p. 195, Oct. 3, 1699; *Acts Privy Council*, vol. ii, no. 732, p. 328; *Calendar State Papers*, vol. xii, no. 315.

[2] *Co391/12*, p. 12; p. 39; *Co5/1287*, p. 416; *Co5/1289*, p. 99.

[3] *Co391/12*, pp. 38, 46.

[4] See discussion of Winthrop *v.* Lechmere, *infra*, chapter v; this case is given as an example in this connection by Dickerson, *American* Colonial Government, p. 276.

and Newcastle it was not much of a factor in the government. The Board was abolished in 1782.

There were other imperial agencies upon which the Council drew for aid as well as upon the Board of Trade. Questions were referred and reports received from the lords of the admiralty, the treasury, the commissioners of customs. The attorney general and solicitor general were called upon when advice was wished. In religious matters the aid of the Bishop of London was requested. After 1718 the position of consulting attorney or "King's Counsel" was created. The position was held by Richard West, Francis Fane, Matthew Lamb and at the opening of the American Revolution Richard Jackson was serving. These men had some influence in shaping the imperial control, particularly over colonial legislation which had to do with judicial procedure.[1]

Enough has been said to show that the King in Council was the center of the imperial system for the control of the administration of justice. Cooperating with the Council, but always subordinate to it, were the other imperial agencies. The whole machinery included the King in Council which registered all final actions, the committee which acted in the capacity of a court of appeals and the Board of Trade which gathered material for investigation. The Council was at once an executive and a judicial body. In its executive capacity it could control the organization and development of the colonial judicial system and in its judicial capacity it was the court of last resort for all cases arising in colonial courts.

The method of review of cases coming on appeal from the colonial courts by the King in Council served a double purpose in the imperial control of colonial judicial matters. It gave the Council the opportunity to correct technical lapses

[1] See Dickerson, p. 75.

of the colonial courts in matters of procedure and it permitted the Council to review a case on its merits where no question of procedure was involved. This shows us that the decisions in cases on appeal, as stated previously, were of two kinds. There were first those decisions in which an attempt was made to control the judicial procedure and administration in the colonies, and there were those in which, after a careful review of the facts in the case, the decision was made on the merits of these facts and no technical question of legal administration was involved.

Several cases will serve to illustrate the more general method of the regulation of colonial courts by decisions of the Council. Edward Plampin, an administrator to one John Baynall of the colony of Virginia, complained that he was entitled to recover five thousand pounds upon a bond given by one Edmund Scarborrow. The suit has been pending for three years because of the influence of the Scarborrow interests which were able to delay justice. Plampin had not been able to bring the case to trial and petitioned the home government. The committee of the Privy Council reported December 18, 1685, that the council should refer the matter by letter to the governor of Virginia and order that the petitioner's cause be speedily brought to trial and determination.[1] The petition of Henry Flint of Cambridge, Massachusetts, for liberty to appeal from a judgment of the general court of trials at Newport, touching his right to a part of an estate left by Thomas Willett, his grandfather, was referred to the committee for appeals July 1, 1718. The following month the committee recommended the dismissal of the case as the proceedings were erroneous and without form and as the judgment had not been regularly given. It was evident that the petitioner

[1] *Acts Privy Council,* vol. ii, no. 203, p. 90; *Calendar State Papers,* vol. vii, no. 2126, p. 508.

could not be relieved in the way he requested without the commencement of a new suit. However, the committee recommended that an appeal should be granted him and the judgment of the lower court reversed. This was accordingly ordered, August 27, 1718.[1] From New York Valentine Cruger petitioned for a speedy hearing of his appeal from a judgment of the governor and council of New York given in a case touching matters of account between the petitioner and Abraham Depeyster. The committee reported that in the proceedings at New York the record had not "been removed up by the proper persons" from the supreme court to the court of the governor and council. Therefore, they were of the opinion that the judgment of the governor and council of New York should be declared null and void but that at the same time the appeal should be dismissed so far as it related to the judgment of the governor and council, that the appellant should be at liberty to renew proceedings in due form before the governor and council of New York. This was so ordered December 21, 1699.[2]

The home government refused to permit the use of general verdicts. In 1729 the petition of one Eunice Wharton, the widow and devisee of William Wharton of the parish of St. Bartholomew, London, from a judgment relating to land and delivered against her in the general court of trials at Newport, Rhode Island, was received and referred to the committee.[3] In March of the next year the committee reported that the judgment appealed from was founded on general verdicts, and the lords postponed any decision in the matter, but ordered that a search be made to see what precedents there were of appeals of this kind, and

[1] *Acts Privy Council*, vol. ii, no. 1298, p. 744.

[2] *Acts Privy Council*, vol. ii, no. 767, p. 345.

[3] *Acts Privy Council*, vol. iii, no. 166; *P. C. 2*, no. 90, p. 436.

that a report be made to the committee.[1] In December the committee restated the proceedings of March and said that search had been made for precedents in the case and the conclusion had been reached that this appeal did properly lie with the Council, notwithstanding the objection that all the evidence given out to the jury was taken down in writing and transmitted as part of the record. The merits of the case were then gone into and the conclusion reached that the verdict or judgment should be set aside and a new trial ordered. In this new trial all the evidence which was offered was to be taken down in writing and if any objection should be made against any of the evidence, such objections together with the resolutions of the court upon the objections were to be taken down in writing, the whole made part of the record and liberty given either side to appeal from the judgment given in the new trial.[2]

In 1740 the petition of the executors of one William Dawkins of London for the hearing of an appeal from a judgment of the general court of Virginia was referred to the committee on appeals.[3] Three years later the committee reported that counsel had been heard and a search had been directed to be made in the Council books to see whether appeals from general verdicts when the evidence had not been taken down in writing had ever been allowed.[4] Two years later, November 28, 1745, the appeal was dismissed in accordance with the report of the committee, it having appeared that the petition of appeal was brought from a judgment founded on a general verdict and that the matters given in evidence on the trial of the action were not transmitted under the seal of the colony.[5]

[1] *Privy Council Register, P. C. 2* no. 91, pp. 192, 257.

[2] *Privy Council Register, P. C. 2*, no. 91, pp. 302-303.

[3] *Privy Council Register, P. C. 2*, no. 95, p. 663.

[4] *Privy Council Register, P. C. 2*, no. 97, p. 384.

[5] *Privy Council Register, P. C. 2*, no. 99, pp. 256, 268.

The general use of affidavits as evidence in court received the distinct disapproval of the Privy Council. This may be seen from the discussion aroused by the case of Rogers *v.* Spalding, which had come to the home government from the Virginia courts.[1] William Rogers, one of the three chief merchants of the Royal African Company, died at Whydah after making a will previous to his departure from England in which his whole estate was left to Sarah Rogers, his sister, and she was named administratrix thereof. Spalding took charge of Rogers' goods at Whydah and refused to give an account except to one Edward Stephens, one of the company's three chief merchants. Sarah Rogers and Mr. George Hume who was with Rogers at his death appeared before the Lord Mayor of London and made affidavits to the facts in the case according to 5 George II for the more easy recovery of debts in the plantations. These affidavits with the proper certificates and a letter of attorney were sent to Virginia and action was brought against Spalding, a legal resident of that province. The Virginia court would not allow the affidavits to be read in evidence and gave judgment with costs against Sarah Rogers.[2] From this judgment she appealed July 10, 1740. It was decided that the affidavits offered in evidence by the petitioner were strictly legal but that as the merits of the case were never laid before the Court, the verdict and judgment should be set aside and the appellant should be at liberty to proceed to another trial on such evidence as she could procure.[3]

Throughout the colonial period the King in Council was the center for the administration of justice in the American colonies. Assistance was had from all the other imperial

[1] *Acts Privy Council*, vol. iii, no. 487.

[2] *Privy Council Register, P. C. 2*, no. 96, pp. 112-116.

[3] *P. C. 2*, no. 96, pp. 110, 135; *Acts Privy Council*, vol. iii, no. 487.

agencies. By decision in cases on appeal the Council could correct and modify judicial procedure in the colonies. As will be seen, the cases coming on appeal brought the home government in close contact with the many-sided activities of the colonies and forced a definite judicial position in many of the confused situations.

CHAPTER III

Appeals to the King in Council

1684-1745

In the first period in which colonial appeals reached the crown the adjustment of the English Government to the new system is very evident. On the other hand the simplicity of the colonial judicial structure is to be noted. And the general distrust on the part of the people for the colonial judiciary is shown by the appeals for the correction of what was considered the most obvious infringement of the attributes of justice. The usual subjects for litigation appear to be those which have to do with the settlement of estates and disposal of property by will as well as the perfecting of title to land. Along with these go a large number of cases in which the appellants feel that there has been a flagrant miscarriage of justice and bring appeals in order that the home government may show its disapproval of any but the traditional judicial policy of respected England.

The complaints concerning the miscarriage of justice are of various kinds. From New York there was a petition complaining of the great delay of justice in cases depending before the governor.[1] To overcome what seemed to him a petty display of provincial spite Captain Christopher Billop petitioned the King in Council concerning a judgment given against him in New York. In 1682, when com-

[1] Petition of Abraham Gouvenor, March 10, 1716. *Acts Privy Council*, vol. ii, no. 1251, p. 708.

mander of the ketch *Deptford,* he had seized an interloper called the *Providence* which was later condemned in the admiralty court of Nevis. Some time after, he consigned a cargo consisting of some negroes and other goods from Nevis to New York, which were, as he thought, illegally seized and judgment in the sum of 1140 pounds was thereupon given against him in the New York courts. He requested the home government to issue an order commanding the mayor's court of New York to stop all proceedings against him and to send over an appeal that the case might be determined in England.[1] The petition of Joseph Brown of Maryland for liberty to appeal from a judgment of five hundred pounds sterling given against him in the provincial court of Maryland was referred to the committee on appeals November 14, 1723. Brown had appealed over the head of the higher courts of Maryland feeling that justice would not be done him. But here the Privy Council set itself on record against irregular procedure. On January 22, 1724, the committee assented that Lord Baltimore should be allowed a copy of the petition and should lay before the committee as quickly as possible any suggestions which he might be able to make on the case. In February, on Lord Baltimore's representation that the case was not yet regularly before the King in Council for an appeal because the regular procedure had not been followed in the colonial courts, it was ordered that the petitioner should be allowed to bring his case by writ of error in a regular manner to the Maryland Court of Appeals.[2]

In cases of delay in the transmitting of proceedings the home government was unusually lenient. Thomas Brooke petitioned in 1730 that the appeal of one Michael Mac-

[1] *Acts Privy Council,* vol. ii, no. 200, p. 89. *Calendar of State Papers,* Colonial Series, vol. vii, pp. 489, 515.

[2] *Acts Privy Council,* vol. iii, no. 54.

namara from the judgment of the court of appeals and error in Maryland be dismissed for non-prosecution.[1] The committee to which the petition was referred, finding that the appeal had not been prosecuted, though admitted for more than a year and a half, recommended its dismissal with five pounds costs. But in December a petition of Macnamara stated that all proceedings had been duly transmitted and asked that an early date might be appointed to hear and determine his appeal. In May, 1731, the case was heard and the judgments reversed, Macnamara being restored to all he had lost by the decisions in the colonial courts.[2] In July, 1733, on report of the committee an appeal of Jahleel Brenton was dismissed for non-prosecution but the case was revived again in 1734 and, Brenton having died in the meantime, the appeal was ordered to be put " in the same condition as at Brenton's death " in order that it might be heard upon its merits.[3]

There was some complaint against the judicial method employed in the colonial courts. The home government was insistent that English method of procedure and traditional legal practice should be maintained. This was particularly true in matters with regard to the examination of evidence and in those concerning the maintenance of the jury system. This attitude was made use of by dissatisfied persons to insist upon a rigid supervision of the provincial courts by the King in Council.

In 1735 the committee reported to the Council that in an action heard at Williamsburg in Virginia, evidence of deeds of lease and release had been offered and that they had been proven as the law required, but that the court refused to

[1] *Acts Privy Council,* vol. iii, no. 215.

[2] *Ibid.*

[3] *Acts Privy Council,* vol. iii, no. 266.

allow them to be offered in evidence to the jury, insisting that the deeds appeared to be cancelled and that no consideration was proven to have been paid. The committee recommended that, as they had heard all the parties and it seemed that the deeds of lease and release ought to have been admitted, the judgment in the general court of Virginia should be reversed.[1] A group of merchants, petitioning from Massachusetts, claimed damages from the sheriff of Middlesex County because his under-sheriff had refused to execute a writ at the petitioner's suit and as a consequence had caused them considerable inconvenience and loss.[2]

English subjects living outside the colonies, particularly the merchant class, availed themselves of the opportunity offered by the system of appeals to remonstrate against colonial methods and to request the home government to correct the more obvious injustices. Ordinarily the home government was expected to be rather partial to the English subject as against the colonial. But there are no evidences that decisions were not reached upon a strictly impartial basis.

The time having elapsed in which an appeal might be made, one John Taylor of London, a merchant, petitioned that notwithstanding the lapse of time he might be admitted to an appeal from the provincial court of Maryland in a case involving the settlement of an estate. The committee to whom the matter was referred recommended that the appeal be admitted provided that the governor and council of Maryland had no legal objection to this proceeding; if they had any such objection they were to return an account to the Privy Council who would then determine the

[1] *Ibid.*, no. 265; P. C. 2, no. 92, pp. 142, 153, 539; P. C. 2, no. 93, pp. 84, 89-90, 100.

[2] *Acts Privy Council,* vol. iii. no. 296.

matter.[1] Thomas Darvall petitioned for a consideration from a judgment given against him in the general court of assizes held for the city of New York, but the King in Council confirmed the judgment of the New York Court after the lords of trade and plantations had considered the petition and reported upon it.[2] In 1738 a London merchant, one Thomas Brown, petitioned from a decision of the lieutenant governor of New York in a court of probate, by which the administration of the estate in New York of John Caswell of London, also a merchant, was granted to Frederick Philips, Esquire. The committee reported, December 15, 1739, and on the twenty-seventh the order in council was given that, no appearance having been entered for the respondent, the case had been heard *ex parte* and the decree affirmed and the appeal dismissed. The decree granted administration of Caswell's estate to Philips, who was only a simple contract creditor for a small sum in comparison with Brown's bond debt. Brown had wished that the administration should be granted to himself.[3]

Protests also reached the home government from merchants who complained that the colonial governments used the trade laws as pretexts for the seizure and condemnation of ships.[4] Generally, however, the petitions asked only the liberty to appeal from what seemed in England judgments wrongly given in colonial courts and had largely to do with the settlement of land titles.[5]

[1] *Acts Privy Council,* vol. ii, no. 1019. Order of April 29, 1707.

[2] *Acts Privy Council,* vol. ii, p. 19, no. 32. *Calendar State Papers,* vol. vi, no. 79, p. 314.

[3] *Acts Privy Council,* vol. iii, no. 454.

[4] *Acts Privy Council,* vol. ii, no. 1269. Petition of Thomas Summers setting forth the seizure and condemnation in New York of the ship, *Good Intent.*

[5] *Acts Privy Council,* vol. iii, no. 233.

In difficulties involving the merchant class when amounts of money were involved, the committee adopted the plan of appointing merchants resident in London to whom the question of the accounts could be submitted for arbitration. Such was the method adopted concerning the petition of Giles Dulake Tidmarsh, the surviving partner and executor of Samuel Appleton, deceased, for the hearing of his appeal from a judgment of the superior court at Boston in August 1733, in favor of a Joseph Brandon and relating to the settlement of an account of the sum of 1634 pounds, 5 shillings and 3 pence which, it was claimed, was due Appleton from Brandon. On June 3, 1736, the committee reported that both sides had agreed to refer the account in question to the examination of merchants resident in London. Thereupon it was ordered by the Council that the parties should draw up their agreement in writing and lay the same before the committee at their next meeting together with the names of such merchants as they should propose to be appointed commissioners for examining into and settling the accounts.

The case was referred, June 7, 1736, by the consent of all parties to Sir John Barnard and Mr. Thomas Sandford on the behalf of the appellants and Mr. Alderman Willimot and Samuel Holden, Esq., on behalf of the respondents to take an account of all the dealings and transactions between Appleton or his executor Tidmarsh and the respondent Brandon. These referees were given the right to examine witnesses on oath in such manner as the referees or any two of them should direct. They were to have access to all books of accounts, papers, writings relating to the matters in question, or true copies of so much as related thereto. They were to proceed upon four days' notice in the matter. All further directions were reserved by the Council until the report should be made by these referees. In July one referee, Samuel Holden, who declined to act, was dropped by consent of both parties and in his place one Silas Hooper was named. These referees heard the facts in the case from both parties and reported back to the Privy Council. In accordance with the report it was ordered that the judgment of the Massachusetts court be reversed, that the action brought by Brandon be dismissed and that a sum of 521 pounds, 1 shilling, 7 pence current money of New England be paid by Brandon to Tidmarsh.[1]

This case was settled according to a precedent established by an earlier case in 1724. In that year a group of London residents, by name Sarah Perry, Micajah Perry and Philip Perry, had petitioned from a sentence of the general court of Virginia in favor of the executors of the estate of Colonel William Randolph, deceased. The Randolphs entered an appearance by Mr. Ellison, an attorney of Symond's Inn, June 30, 1724. In November of that year the committee of the Privy Council, having heard both sides, ordered the parties to agree upon commissioners on each side for sealing the accounts in question in the appeal and reporting on the matter within a week. The parties named Humphrey Morrice and George Newport for the the appellants, Robert Wilmont and John Faulker for the respondents, and the committee agreed to the naming of these. The committee then ordered that these commissioners or any two of them, on giving four days' notice should proceed to examine the accounts and that the appellants should leave with the commissioners from time to time all books of accounts, letters, papers and writings, relating to the matter in question.

In March of the following year, a doubt having arisen as to whether the whole accounts from the beginning or

[1] *Acts Privy Council*, vol. iii, no. 319, pp. 428-430.

only the articles of insurance and interest involved were to be considered by the commissioners, the committee declared that the articles of insurance and interest alone were to be dealt with. In July, the commissioners reported and the committee recommended that the judgment of the colonial court was erroneous and recommended that it be reversed and judgment entered for the appellants to the amount of 2460 pounds damages and ten pounds costs to be recovered from the assets of the late Colonel Randolph, if possible, otherwise out of the proper goods of the respondents.[1]

Two other interesting cases involving disputes as to mercantile accounts should be noted.[2] The first was a petition of William Hunt, a merchant, "for a short day" for the hearing of his appeal from the judgment of the royal court of Virginia given in his action against the executors of the estate of William Clopton for the recovery of 1094 pounds, 16 shillings and 11 pence. This was due to the petitioner, it was claimed, as a balance in the partnership between him and Clopton. The petition reached the Privy Council and was referred to the committee, January 12, 1738.

In the discussion of the case the petitioner set forth that at Clopton's death their partnership account had not been settled. In February, 1733, there was due William Hunt, according to his account, 973 pounds, 3 shillings and 11 pence to which he added interest at 5 per cent to the date of his petition. The jury after several trials refused to allow the petitioner any part of the interest he had charged and the court refused to direct the jury whether they should or should not allow the petitioner a moiety of the duty paid by him on tobacco sold to merchants who had later proved to be insolvent. The jury finally decided that the first penny only of the duties could be allowed but would not take it upon

[1] *Acts Privy Council*, vol. iii, no. 65.

[2] *Acts Privy Council*, vol. iii, no. 427; *ibid.*, no. 545.

themselves to determine whether the petitioner should be granted this, since the court declined to give an opinion.[1] The committee reported that the verdict should be affirmed except that the method of payment of the currency debt by an assignment of a moiety of the outstanding debts of the partnership should not be tolerated; this portion of the verdict was therefore reversed.[2]

Also from Virginia came the petition of Edward Randolph in May 1742 asking to be admitted to an appeal from the courts of Virginia concerning an account between himself and William Beverly.[3] In March 1744 the lieutenant governor and council of Virginia sent a representation stating that Randolph had misrepresented the proceedings of the general court of the colony in his petition and asked that the king should make a decision agreeable to "his wonted tenderness and care" for his subjects in order that justice might be done. The next year, July 18, 1745, the appeal was dismissed.

Appeals involving the settlement of estates show the tendency of the home government to have been toward the maintenance in the colonies of the essential features of the English land system. Especially is this true in the matter of entailed estates. The imperial attitude was to maintain entailed estates while the colonial position shows a tendency in some instances away from this policy. In the cases coming on appeal to the home government concerning the disposal of estates the King in Council worked laboriously over the many involved and conflicting claims in order that an impartial judicial decision based upon English law might be reached.

[1] *Privy Council Register, P. C. 2,* no. 96, pp. 175, 234, 235-40.

[2] *P. C. 2,* no. 96, p. 263.

[3] *Acts Privy Council,* vol. iii, p. 546.

A case concerning the will of Herbert Pelham reached the home government in 1737. Pelham died in the year 1673 leaving as issue his sons Waldegrave, Edward, Henry and a daughter Penelope. The original ejectment was brought by a descendant of the elder Pelham against a group of people to recover possession of a tract of land involved in the will and containing seven hundred acres of land and upwards located in Massachusetts Bay. After several postponements the committee took the case into consideration November 17, 1738. The counsel for the appellant offered in the course of evidence to read out of their proceedings an exemplification of the will of Herbert Pelham dated 1672 under the seal of the prerogative court of Canterbury. The respondents objected to this, insisting that "the exemplification of a will from Doctors Commons" could not be read as evidence in a case involving real estate in the colony of Massachusetts Bay. The committee decided to agree with the respondents and recommended the dismissal of the appeal.[1] Another appeal against citizens of Massachusetts to recover tracts of land amounting to some 2000 pounds under this same will was dismissed for the same reason.[2]

There were a large number of cases involving the settlement of estates carried on appeal to the Privy Council. From Virginia Robert D'Oyly complained of the management by the governor of the estates of his brother, Capt. D'Oyly, who had died intestate.[3] A Philip Ludwell brought before the Privy Council by appeal the matter of a suit against him by one John Toton. This case involved certain actions of Sir William Berkeley as the governor of Virginia, because Ludwell had married the executrix of

[1] *Acts Privy Council,* vol. iii, no. 414.

[2] Pelham *v.* Bannister *et al, Acts Privy Council,* vol. iii, no. 428; March 22, 1739.

[3] *Acts Privy Council,* vol. ii, no. 1100, p. 607.

the Berkeley estate. A question was raised as to the jurisdiction of the general court of Virginia. This question was whether the court could proceed in an action against the executors of the estate for things done by the testator, for which he could not be sued in his lifetime without a special commision, since Berkeley was accountable as governor to none but the King.[1] From South Carolina William Bowtell and Thomas Wenborne appealed to the Privy Council concerning a debt owing from Seth Sothell, governor of South Carolina. Sothell had died in Virginia leaving as sole executrix his widow, who married John Lear, a member of the council of Virginia. Sothell's widow died leaving all the personal estate to Lear. Lear refused to pay Sothell's debts. As Lear was a member of the council in Virginia he took advantage of a rule that none of the council should be liable to any action whatever and no process in law could touch the persons of the councillors or their estates. The colonial court refused to entertain any suit against Lear. The appellants prayed that Lear might not be protected by any such "contrivance", but that they might have the same remedy against him as though he were not of the Council.[2] From Massachusetts in 1718 Christopher Taylor of Boston requested liberty to appeal from the decree of the judge of probate of wills, confirmed by the governor and council, approving a will made by his father after he was deprived of his reason, whereby the stepmother and her daughter became the executors.[3] An appeal involving the division of the real estate of Samuel Clark of Connecticut was under consideration from November 1737

[1] *Acts Privy Council,* vol. ii, no. 393, p. 184; *Calendar State Papers,* vol. viii, no. 1259.

[2] *Acts Privy Council,* vol. ii, no. 632, p. 299; *Calendar State Papers,* vol. x, no. 46.

[3] *Acts Privy Council,* vol. ii, no. 1302, p. 748.

until July 1745, but was finally dismissed without anything being accomplished.[1]

The question of entailed estates in the colonies was reviewed by the home govenment in two rather intricate cases. In March, 1743, David Meade of Virginia petitioned for the hearing of his appeal from the judgment given by the general court of Virginia April 15, 1742. This judgment was concerning an ejectment filed against the petitioner by William Thrustout, as lessee, under Martha Goodwin and others, for the recovery of one messuage, one tenement, and nine hundred acres of land with the appurtenances in the parish of Newport and county of the Isle of Wight in Virginia. Judgment was given November 3, 1743, for the appellant with costs and possession of the estate restored to him. This decision was given because of the following facts in the case. Letters patent for the estate had been issued July 10, 1680, to Colonel John Lear. His son Thomas predeceased his father leaving three children, John, Elizabeth and Martha. The estate in question descended in tail to John Lear the grandson, who by indenture of lease sold it to the petitioner. Sometime later John Lear died, whereby the estate tail determined, even if it had till that time subsisted.[2]

The other case involving entailed estate is that of Burgess *v* Hack. On December 27, 1737, Ferdinando John Paris, as solicitor, entered an appearance in England for Mr. John Hack of Virginia to the appeal of Frances Burgess, a widow.[3] On February 21, 1737, the King in Council re-

[1] *Acts Privy Council*, vol. iii, no. 422.

[2] *Acts Privy Council*, vol. iii, no. 568; *P. C. 2*, no. 386; *ibid.*, no. 98, pp. 27-30.

[3] Burgess *v* Hack or Gulliver *v.* Hack. Hardwicke Papers. *British Museum Additional MSS.*, no. 36216, folio 102; *Acts Privy Council*, vol. iii, no. 391, p. 530. Gulliver was the lessee of the land claimed by Mrs. Burgess and in the Virginia courts the case is known as Gulliver *v.* Hack.

ferred to the committee the petition of Frances Burgess for her lessee Lemuel Gulliver for "a short day" for hearing the appeal from the judgment of the general court of pleas in Virginia, in favor of John Hack in an ejectment brought against Hack in the name of Gulliver for the recovery of ten messuages and 2266 acres of land with their appurtenances claimed by Mrs. Burgess. The committee reported back in November of the same year saying that the proceedings in the Virginia court had been defective because it did not state how Frances Burgess became the heir-at-law of the original owner of the land, one David Fox. Because this seemed a material fact and necessary to be determined before a report could be made it was thought that the record should be sent back to the Virginia court, which was to determine how and when Frances Burgess, lessor of the land to Lemuel Gulliver, became the heir-at-law of the original testator David Fox. And in case the parties could not agree upon the facts a jury was to decide the matter and their decision established and made part of the case. The Virginia court was ordered to give the proper and necessary directions for carrying this order into execution and the record to be returned as soon as possible. The committee heard counsel for both sides during the month of November, 1737.

The case involved the question of the entailed estate left by David Fox at his death under a will dated November 4, 1660, and the final disposition of the estate by his descendants.[1] David Fox died in November, 1669, and his estate was divided by a will dated November 4, 1660. He left the one plantation, upon which he lived, to his wife Anne during her life time and then to his son David. Another plantation and the land in question in the suit

[1] Hardwicke Papers, *British Museum Additional MSS.*, no. 36216, folio 105.

he left to his son William and his daughter Elizabeth by another marriage to be equally divided by them when they became twenty-one years of age or on the day of the marriage of his daughter if this should happen first. In case of the death of one of them the land was to be the property of the survivor.[1] After the death of the father William and Elizabeth possessed themselves of the premises by virtue of their father's will. William died before he was twenty-one and the premises passed to Elizabeth. She married Peter Hack and had one son Nicholas Hack, her only heir. Nicholas Hack occupied the estate and enjoyed the use of it until his death. He left the property by will to his two brothers, John and Spencer Hack, by another marriage. John Hack therefore possessed himself of the estate at the death of Nicholas, the brother Spencer having previously died without issue. But Frances Burgess was advised that the will of David Fox created an estate tail in moieties to William and Elizabeth Fox with cross remainders in tail. Since both William and Elizabeth were dead without issue, Frances Burgess now declared that she was

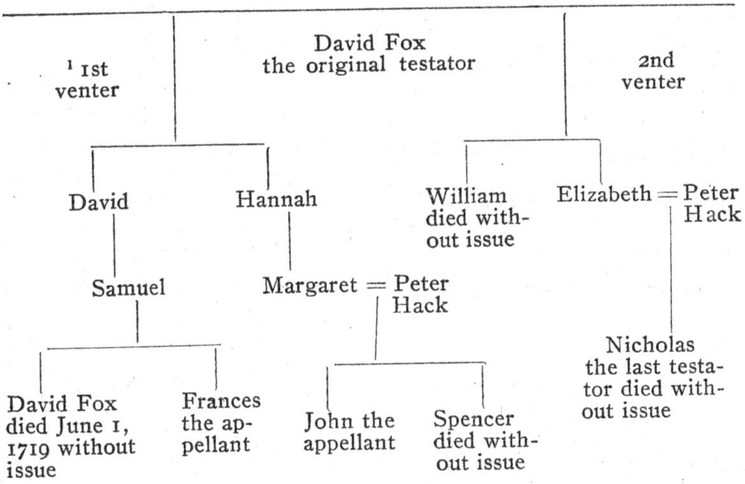

the heir-at-law to the testator David Fox and as such and under the original will entitled to the 2266 acres of land. She brought the action of ejectment in the general court of pleas in Virginia in the name of Lemuel Gulliver, her lessee, against John Hack in order to recover the estate with its appurtenances.

The respondent answered the action in the Virginia courts, and when the case was tried the parties waived the trial of the issue by a jury and agreed upon a case in lieu of a special verdict. They agreed upon the facts as stated and added that David Fox had at the time of his death two other daughters, Hannah and Rebecca, by his first marriage. Hannah's daughter Mary had married Peter Hack after the death of Elizabeth and had issue in the persons of John Hack, the defendant, and Spencer, deceased. On April 15, 1736, the Virginia court decided that the law was with the defendant and against the claims of Lemuel Gulliver. The defendant was given costs against Frances Burgess as lessor of Gulliver.

When the case reached the Privy Council the facts as presented were considered erroneous and, as has been said, the case was sent back to the Virginia court to show how Frances Burgess became heir-at-law to David Fox. The general court of Virginia, pursuant to this direction of the lords of the committee, ordered that all parties should appear on October 15, 1738, in order that the record might be amended as the committee wished. The parties appeared, but disagreed upon the state of facts in the case, and the court ordered that this should be settled by a jury on the first day of the next court. Accordingly, a jury was sworn to settle the facts and upon their oaths found the following: that Frances Burgess was the sister and heir-at-law of her brother David Fox, the great grandson of the original testator; at the death of her brother, which occurred June

1, 1719, Frances became the heir-at-law of her brother and at the same time of the original testator, her great grandfather. With these facts the appeal now came to the Privy Council for final determination on its merits.

The appellants asked that the judgment of the general court of Virginia should be reversed with costs on the ground that William and Elizabeth, under the will of David Fox, took only an estate tail in moieties with cross remainder in tail to each other with the reversion in fee to the heir of the testator. After the death of William without issue, Elizabeth had an estate in tail general in the whole. There having happened a failure of issue of both William and Elizabeth by the death of Nicholas Hack without children, the reversion in fee descended then upon the appellant, Frances, as heir-at-law of the original testator and Nicholas Hack had no right to divide the premises of the original plantation. Both parties pressed the case vigorously and employed solicitors of ability to represent them; but the intricacies of the case made it drag along until finally it disappeared without the judgment of the Virginia court being reversed and probably with a family adjustment in the colony.

The dismissal of the appeals growing out of the series of cases arising from the will and the disposal of the property of Jonathan Waldo of Massachusetts throws some light on colonial procedure and its review in England.[1] Samuel Waldo of Boston appealed from a judgment of the superior court at Boston of August 8, 1732, given in an action in which Waldo had attempted to recover from Thomas Fairweather possession of all the deeds and writings of his father, Jonathan Waldo, deceased. Also he appealed from a decree of the governor and council of Massachusetts Bay of January 13, 1732, affirming a judgment of the probate

[1] *Acts Privy Council*, vol. iii, nos. 272, 295, 321, 325.

court of that colony by which Fairweather was not compelled to deliver up the books of accounts, notes, bonds and mortgages belonging to the estate of Jonathan Waldo. On February 28, 1733, the committee recommended that the appeals be admitted on the usual security, and in March of that year William Parkin and Joshua Channing entered into security of one hundred pounds in each of the two suits for Waldo's prosecution of his appeals. In May a petition of Samuel Waldo asking for "a short day" for hearing these two appeals was referred to the committee. The committee appointed the first meeting in January to hear both appeals. In March, 1734, the committee ordered that, as Thomas Fairweather had died since the case was started, the appeals of Samuel Waldo be revived against the executors of his father's estate, namely, Hannah and John Fairweather. In November, 1734, it was decided that the two revived appeals would be heard on December 10, 1734. At that time the committee recommended that the judgments of the Massachusetts court be affirmed and the appeal denied.[1]

The first petition set forth that Waldo, being absent at the time of his father's death, the executors proved the will of Jonathan Waldo before Joshua Willard, judge of the probate of wills, and that Thomas Fairweather as one of the executors possessed himself of all the testator's books of account, promissory notes, bonds and mortgages. Soon after the arrival in New England of Samuel Waldo he accepted the administration of the estate which had been given him in his absence and was denied the books of account by Fairweather. He then applied to the judge of the probate court, but was denied his suit, and from this he appealed to the governor and council, who affirmed the denial of the probate court.

On the twelfth of December the committee reviewed the

[1] *Acts Privy Council*, vol. iii, p. 377.

second petition of Samuel Waldo. This petition set forth that the petitioner, as eldest son and principal heir-at-law of Jonathan Waldo, was absent in England at the time of his father's death. Thomas Fairweather, who married one of his sisters, had possessed himself of the deeds and writings relating to the several estates and refused to give them up. The petitioner brought an action before the justices of the inferior court of Suffolk county against Thomas Fairweather for the recovery of the papers. To this action Fairweather pleaded not guilty and the petitioner demurred. Fairweather attempted then to substitute a second plea but the court declared that the first plea should stand and ordered the case tried by a jury. The jury found for Fairweather costs of the suit and later judgment was given that he should recover these costs. An appeal was taken from this judgment to the superior court of judicature held for the county of Suffolk. In view of the facts in the case the committee recommended that this appeal be upheld and judgments of the lower courts reversed; if the appellant wished he might bring a new action.[1]

In January, 1734, Cornelius Waldo, a merchant of Boston, petitioned for leave to appeal from two judgments, the one in the court of common pleas for the county of Worcester May 8, 1733, and the other in the superior court of Massachusetts September 19, 1733. These judgments were on an action of ejectment brought against his tenants,—Daniel Gookin, Robert Barber and John Alexander in the names of Samuel Waldo, Jonathan Waldo and Thomas Fairweather as executors of the estate of Ann, executrix of the estate of Jonathan Waldo, to obtain possession of 710 acres of land with buildings and appurtenances in the County of Worcester. In January 1734, the appeals were admitted and in April William Parkin, ironmonger, and

[1] *Acts Privy Council*, iii, p. 378.

Joshua Channing, haberdasher, both of London, entered into the security required. The hearing was held in March and at this time the petitioner set forth that he had mortgaged to Jonathan Waldo in fee the farms and land mentioned in the petition in the town of Worcester in Massachusetts under a proviso that the mortgage was to be void on the payment of 1060 pounds to Jonathan Waldo. At the death of Jonathan Waldo his lands passed to his eldest son Samuel; he together with his brother Jonathan and his sister Anne and Thomas Fairweather were the executors. These persons brought an action of ejection against the tenants of the petitioner in the inferior court of common pleas in the county of Worcester to recover possession of the mortgaged premises.[1] The case was heard May 8, 1733, in this inferior court which gave judgment that the plaintiffs should recover against Cornelius Waldo the sum of 1186 pounds to be paid within two months with costs or on failure of payment to recover against the petitioner the possession of the premises sued for with eight pounds, ten shillings, six pence costs. This judgment was confirmed in the superior court of Massachusetts. The committee recommended and it was so ordered that this judgment of the Massachusetts court be altered in such a way that the Waldo heirs should recover possession of the premises sued for and costs of suits in the courts of the province unless Cornelius Waldo should pay to the executors the sum of 1206 pounds in good bills of credit on the province aforesaid or in silver money together with the subsequent interest to be computed upon the principal at six per cent. The altered judgment was to be entered in the superior court of Massachusetts and was to stand as the judgment in this cause.[2]

[1] *Acts Privy Council*, vol. iii, p. 405.

[2] *Acts Privy Council*, vol. iii, pp. 406-407.

The heirs of Jonathan Waldo also brought an action of ejectment against John Waldo of Boston, a distiller, to obtain the possession of a piece of land and still house in Boston with two stills and all the appurtenances belonging to them. This was brought to England on appeal in November, 1734. In March, 1735, the committee recommended that no appeal be granted. The case as reviewed before the committee brought out some interesting facts. The petitioner, John Waldo, had mortgaged in fee simple the premises involved in the suit to Jonathan Waldo. This mortgage was to be void on payment of 250 pounds to Jonathan Waldo, his heirs or executor on or before March 6, 1729. At the death of Jonathan Waldo the property went to his eldest son Samuel Waldo with the executors as noted before. An action of ejectment was brought June 9, 1733, against the petitioner in the inferior court of common pleas in Boston in the name of the executors. Samuel Waldo, as one of the plaintiffs, disavowed this action and the other parties plaintiff declared that they would maintain it without him. At the session of the court held July 3, 1733, the petitioner was required to plead to issue. When he refused, judgment was given against him for the sum of 315 pounds, 12 shillings, 6 pence, to be paid in two months, with 5 pounds, 4 shillings, 6 pence costs, or in default of this the mortgaged property was to pass to the executors of the estate. The case was heard on appeal in the superior court of Massachusetts. Here judgment was given that the petitioner should give up the premises sued for together with 16 pounds, 8 shillings costs or the petitioner should pay outright 320 pounds. From this last judgment the petitioner moved for an appeal to the King in Council.[1]

The final appearance of the Waldo estate before the home

[1] *Acts Privy Council*, vol. iii, pp. 431-432.

government came in three petitions of Samuel Waldo that his three appeals from judgments given upon actions brought (a) by Thomas and Hannah Fairweather, (b) by his brother Jonathan Waldo and (c) by Edward and Ann Tyng against the appellant to render an account of all the money in his hands belonging to his father Jonathan Waldo, deceased, be heard by the Council. These petitions were referred to the committee December 19, 1734.[1] These appeals had to do with the final settlement of the estate and the division of the property into equal shares. When the first of these cases came on appeal to the superior court of Massachusetts in August 1733, that tribunal confirmed the judgment of the lower court and said that Thomas and Hannah Fairweather should recover against the petitioner the sum of 3046 pounds, 1 shilling and 2¾ pence with costs at 9 pounds, 5 shillings. The committee recommended that this appeal be dismissed March 20, 1735, and that the judgments of both the lower and the superior courts be affirmed. There were no exceptions taken in the courts below for want of parties and there were two other actions heard at the same time in the superior court which were of a like nature and brought by the executors of the estate. On April 3, 1735, the King in Council by an order dismissed the three appeals.[2]

Land cases were of various kinds.[3] Generally they concerned the conflicting claims resulting from the settlement of the colonies and the overlapping boundaries of the very early grants. They involved also the right of a proprietor to dispose of an estate by grant or the right of a legislative assembly to vote such a grant. The general con-

[1] *Acts Privy Council*, vol. iii, no. 325.

[2] *Ibid.*, pp. 451-452.

[3] *Acts Privy Council*, vol. ii, p. 446, no. 909; vol. ii, no. 110; vol. ii, no. 800; vol. iii, no. 421; vol. iii, no. 476.

fusion in matters of land transfers resulting from the growth and development of a primitive community was reflected in these appeals to the King in Council.

There was, for instance, the appeal of Thomas Allen, 1706, from the superior conrt at Boston confirming the verdict of an inferior Massachusetts court at Waldo in favor of Humphrey Spencer and involving an old original grant from Sir Ferdinando Gorges.[1] Benjamin Tasker, upon an action of trespass and ejectment by John Simpson for the recovery of 1000 acres of plantable land lying in Queen's County, Maryland, brought in 1739 the question of a land grant from the lord proprietor of Maryland before the Privy Council. It was shown that the land in question had been granted by the proprietor in 1640 to Giles Brent and his heirs. Simpson had come into possession of the land through a descendant of Giles Brent, one William Brent. The appeal was dismissed and the judgment of the colonial court allowed to stand.[2] Objecting to the decision of the general assembly in Connecticut, Robert Wheeler appealed, in 1737, for the recovery of possession of twenty-five acres of land left in the hands of Thomas Levenworth.[3] An appeal on an action of ejectment from Massachusetts concerning mortgaged lands was dismissed with thirty pounds costs.[4] Another relating to the possession of 750 acres of land in Maryland was dismissed for non-prosecution with 10 pounds costs.[5]

The frequency with which these cases were dismissed or lost sight of in the regular business of the Council leads one to think that advantage was taken by the colonists of

[1] *Acts Privy Council*, vol. ii, no. 1006.

[2] *Acts Privy Council*, vol. iii, no. 476.

[3] *Ibid.*, no. 421.

[4] *Ibid.*, no. 409.

[5] *Ibid.*, no. 216.

the distance to England and the general ignorance there of colonial conditions to attempt to get a decision from the home government upon a problem that was intricate enough before the colonial courts. The promptness with which these appeals were dismissed or the judgments of the colonial courts were upheld shows that the lords of the Privy Council recognized this fact. When a case was considered worthy of consideration much time and labor was spent upon it. Of the land cases of the period two, one concerning the appeal of Samuel Allen from New Hampshire and the other concerning the appeal of the Mohegan Indians from Connecticut, are of unusual interest.

The King in Council referred the petition of Samuel Allen, proprietor of New Hampshire, that his appeal be admitted from a verdict given by the superior court of judicature in New Hampshire, to the Board of Trade March 20, 1701.[1] This petition set forth that James I had granted to the Council of New England the land between the fortieth and forty-eighth degrees of latitude; the Council of New England assigned the land to John Mason in New Hampshire who legally conveyed it to Samuel Allen; in 1683 King Charles II made Edward Cranfield governor with instructions that none of the inhabitants were to be dispossessed of land but a quit-rent of six pence per pound for all produce of the land was to be accepted; some of the inhabitants became obstinate and would not pay the quit-rent and the proprietor served actions of ejectment against them and recovered this rent; William Vaughn appealed to the home government concerning this, and after debate it was decided that the proprietor had the right in the matter and this was confirmed by the order in council November 1, 1686. The petitioner then brought action because some of the inhabitants refused to pay their quit-rent, and this action

[1] *Acts Privy Council*, vol. ii, p. 365, no. 818.

coming up in the superior court of New Hampshire against Richard Waldron, the court decided in favor of Waldron and against the proprietor.[1] The petition further stated that the case involved the determination of the proprietor's right to the whole province and that justice was not to be expected in any trial at law held in the province because every inhabitant of the colony was a tenant or a party concerned.

The case was admitted to appeal at Kensington, April 24, 1701, and the officials of the colony were notified.[2] In November, 1701, Allen petitioned again, saying that there had been a delay in the instructions of April 24, that the petitioner could not summon the parties for the December meeting of the Council and that he asked for a delay. This the committee granted in December, naming the first council day of August, 1702, as the day for hearing the appeal and required five hundred pounds as security for the prosecution of the case at that time and the abiding by the decision of the Council. This security was furnished within the next two weeks by John Usher and Whitefield Hayter.

In July, 1702, Waldron petitioned to have the case delayed and this was referred to the Committee for appeals, while within the following fortnight Allen petitioned setting forth the consent of the solicitors of both parties that the case be heard on the first council day in October. The case, however, did not come before the King in Council until December, 1702, at which time it was ordered in accordance with the report from the committee that the judgment of the colonial court be affirmed; but as this judgment was not final in its nature the appellant was to be left at

[1] *CO5/862*, no. 44. Samuel Allen's petition to the King in Council, ordered by His Majesty in Council, referred to Lords Commissioners of Trade and Plantations, March 20, 1700.

[2] *Ibid.*

liberty to bring a new action in ejectment in the courts in New Hampshire in order to try his title as proprietor to the lands in question. If in this new trial any doubts were to arise concerning the evidence given, such doubts were to be specially stated and taken in writing in order that in case either party should think fit to appeal to the Queen in Council from the judgment of the colonial court, she might be more fully informed in order to come to a final determination of the case.[1]

Here the matter rested for three years when Thomas Allen revived it by petitioning that the appeal of his father, Samuel Allen, against the verdict of the superior court be revived in his name, since it had been abated by the death of his father. This petition was granted and the court which should hear the case was ordered to state definitely any doubts concerning the evidence taken, in order that the Council might be fully informed should an appeal be taken to England. The case was heard in the New Hampshire courts in 1707 and brought on appeal to the King in Council the next year, and in the last month of 1708 the committee recommended the dismissal of the appeal, which was ordered accordingly.[2]

A small group of appeals will indicate the attitude of the home government toward the Indians. The possession of tracts of land within the colonies by this race and the continued encroachment of the white settlers upon the rights of the Indians acted as an irritant to both parties. In its judicial hearings the English government attempted an impartial attitude but the disputes had become so involved before they reached the King in Council that a solution of the problems involved was no easy matter. Consequently, we find long periods of delay, with the suspicion developing

[1] *Acts Privy Council*, vol. ii, pp. 366-367.

[2] *Acts Privy Council*, vol. ii, p. 367.

that the English settlers from their position had the benefit of the doubt.

The most famous case of this kind is that of the Mohegan Indians against the governor and company of Connecticut and other possessors of land in the north parish of New London and in the townships of Colchester, Lynne and Hebron.[1] This was given a judicial hearing before the King in Council which was the outcome of a long number of petitions and memorials to the home government.[2] These petitions originated in the period under discussion. In 1703 a complaint had been made by the chief sachem of the Mohegan Indians, and Queen Anne had appointed the governor of Massachusetts Bay together with others to be a commission to examine into the matter and make such determination as should seem agreeable to them. An appeal to Her Majesty in Council was to be allowed from this determination if it was so wished. The determination was made by the commissioners in favor of the Indians and the colony of Connecticut was condemned in costs.

Sir Henry Ashurst, the agent for Connecticut, brought an appeal from the judgment of the commissioners. The part of the judgment which condemned the colony in costs was reversed, but the facts of the case were to be heard by a commission of review under the direction of the governor and council of New York. As this was never carried into effect, the Board of Trade recommended, and it was accordingly ordered, that a new commission consisting of the governor and council of New York and the governor and assistants of Rhode Island be named, the quorum to be not less than five, to review the case, the expenses to be borne by the crown because of the poverty of the Indians.[3]

[1] *Acts Privy Council*, vol. iv, no. 607.

[2] *Acts Privy Council*, vol. iii, no. 392, pp. 531-539; vol. iv, no. 427; *ibid.*, no. 607.

[3] *Acts Privy Council*, vol. iii, pp. 532-533.

In 1739 John and Samuel Mason of New London, Connecticut, petitioned on behalf of the Mohegan Indians, complaining of the proceedings of the commission. The case dragged on with hearings before the Council and the Board of Trade for a year when the committee reported. From the Board of Trade report upon the matter it appeared that the commission had consisted of two commissioners from New York and seven from Rhode Island who had met at Norwich in 1738. This being a commission of review, it seemed that the former judgments and proceedings should have been taken into consideration, but accusation was made that there was no evidence that this had been done. More than this the Indians had not been heard in their own behalf; likewise Samuel Mason, who was the trustee and guardian of the tribe of Indians, and without whose consent the tribe could not alienate their lands, since the legal property thereof was rested in the Mason family as trustee, had not been heard. The members of the commission from New York had been dissatisfied and had protested. But the Rhode Island commissioners had proceeded without them and basing their decision upon two deeds, signed by Ben Uncas, declared to be a chief of the tribe, gave the lands in question to the colony of Connecticut. Because of these deeds the commission declared against the Indians except in the case of one small tract of land.[1]

The committee declared that the proceedings of the Rhode Island Commissioners were very irregular and should be set aside, that another commission of review should be named under the great seal, and that a draft of the instructions with a list of suitable names should be laid before the committee by the Board of Trade.[2] Some time was now taken, the agent for Connecticut petitioning that the new

[1] *Acts Privy Council*, vol. iii, p. 535.

[2] *Acts Privy Council*, vol. iii, p. 536.

commission might include the Rhode Island assistants of the former commission and that the New York councillors might be omitted. The Masons petitioned against this.

A new commission was, however, appointed in 1741 comprising the governor and councillors of New York and New Jersey; liberty was given for an appeal within "a limited time," and the expense of the commission was to be defrayed by the crown.[1] This commission reported in favor of the colony and against the tribe of Indians. Eighty-six of the Mohegan tribe petitioned against this judgment in 1746, asking that so much of the decree as reversed the judgment of the first commission under Joseph Dudley in 1705 be set aside. Again there was a lapse of time in which Mason asked for reimbursement because of money advanced from his private funds and the agent of Connecticut set forth that Mason had received nearly five hundred pounds and should not be helped further under pretence of aiding the Mohegans, as he was really promoting his own private interests.

Finally, in 1756, the committee, stating that as no appearance had been entered for the respondents except for the governor and company of the colony of Connecticut to the appeal of the eighty-six Indians, although thirteen years had elapsed since the decree was given by the commissioners of review, the usual summons might be affixed on the Royal Exchange and in the New England Coffee House.[2] Nothing more was heard of the case until after 1760. At that time, the case was revived by the home government against the heirs of, and others claiming from, such of the respondents as were dead. This was to be done without prejudice to any objection that might be advanced to the appellant's right to revive the appeal. December 2, 1769

[1] *Acts Privy Council,* vol. iii, p. 537.

[2] *Acts Privy Council,* vol. iii, p. 539.

an appearance for the possessors of the lands in Connecticut to the appeal of the Mohegan Indians was entered by Thomas Fife of Basinghall Street. The committee heard counsel in the case several times during the next two years but postponed making a report. In June, 1772, letters were issued to the master of the rolls and Sir Fletcher Norton to attend the committee in the hope that a final determination might be reached. The final decision, however, did not occur until January 15, 1773, at which time the appeal was dismissed, and the judgment of the commissioners of review of 1743 was upheld.[1]

The attitude of the home government toward the Indians is illustrated by another case in the year 1760, which came to the consideration of the Privy Council through the petition of Reuben Cognetew, a Mohegan Indian, complaining that the English inhabitants of Massachusetts Bay had unjustly encroached upon the lands of the Indians and hindered and obstructed them in their fishing rights. This petition was referred to the Board of Trade and upon its report and petition was sent to the governor of Massachusetts Bay who was required to place it before the general court of the province and make an enquiry into the conduct of the persons appointed guardians of this particular tribe. A full report was to be returned to the home government in order that justice might be done the Indians and that they might be secured the quiet possession and peaceable enjoyment of their just rights in the future. The report of the committee of the general court together with a letter of Governor Bernard reached the Privy Council the next year and these were referred to the Board of Trade, which made a representation in the matter on September 10, 1761.[2]

[1] *Acts Privy Council*, vol. iv, no. 607, pp. 723-724; *Acts Privy Council*, vol. v, no. 133.

[2] *Acts Privy Council*, vol. iv, pp. 460-461.

A series of cases shows the attitude of the English judicial system toward ecclesiastical matters in the colonies. Of these the two most interesting come from Rhode Island and turn upon the meaning and definition of the word "orthodox". The question here was whether a Church of England divine or a dissenting minister was to be understood as being an orthodox leader.[1] Another from New York in which the Society for the Propagation of the Gospel became interested led to an order in council dated January 8, 1713, for the admitting of all appeals to the governor and council and thence to the queen in all cases where the clergy were immediately concerned.[2] This order was the result of the Board of Trade representation in the case of Thomas Poyer of New York. Thomas Poyer had been inducted into office as rector of the parish of Jamaica in Long Island by Governor Hunter of New York. But he was kept out of the parsonage by persons "disaffected to the church." Poyer had been unwilling to seek relief at law, because he was apprehensive that if the case were tried by dissenters he would not have justice done him and an appeal would not lie to the Queen in Council because the value involved in the parsonage was small. The Society for the Propagation of the Gospel took up the matter and offered a representation to the Queen in Council concerning the case July 28, 1712. This was referred to the Board of Trade which reported back, with the result that the Council issued the order of January 8.[3]

The first of the Rhode Island appeals relating to ecclesiastical matters was made by Joseph Torrey of South Kingston, Kings County, in December, 1733. The appeal

[1] Torrey *v.* Mumford. *Acts Privy Council,* vol. iii, no. 293; *P. C. 2,* no. 93, pp. 281, 489, 503.

[2] *Acts Privy Council,* vol. ii, p. 665.

[3] *Ibid.*

was from the decision of the inferior court of common pleas in June, 1732, in favor of George Mumford upon an action of trespass and ejectment brought against him by Torrey to recover possession of 280 acres of land, part of a tract of three hundred acres assigned for the use of an orthodox minister for the community.[1] The petition set forth that John Hall and several others of the denomination of christians called Presbyterians, being seized in fee of a large tract of land in the colony known as Petaquamscut purchase, at a meeting on the fourth of June, 1668, agreed that a tract of three hundred acres of the best land in a convenient place in the purchase should be laid out and forever set apart as an encouragement for the development of religious thought. The income and improvement of this tract should therefore be preserved for a person in the settlement who should be orthodox and who might preach God's word to all the inhabitants. The three hundred acres were accordingly laid out and alloted to and for the use of the ministry and this was entered upon record in December, 1679, in these words: "For the ministry three hundred acres".

At a meeting of the proprietors of this purchase held in 1692 for the further settling and confirming other lands it was agreed and ordered that the surveyor, a Mr. John Smith, should enter the word "ministry" upon the original plot of the purchase in the acres reserved for that purpose. The three hundred acres thus set aside for the use of the Presbyterian ministry were occupied in 1702 by the Reverend Samuel Miles, a Presbyterian, who was chosen by the people of Kingston, or King's Town, to preach the gospel among them and who upon entering into the office was put into possession of 280 acres, part of the three hundred acres of

[1] *P. C. 2*, no. 93, pp. 281, 489-504.

the said ministerial lands, and held and enjoyed the same, receiving the rents and profits of these for several years.

The Reverend Mr. Miles removed from Kingston in 1714 and entered into an agreement to lease the land to one James Bundy who executed a bond to redeliver possession to Samuel Miles or any other person entrusted with his interest in it. Joseph Torrey, who was the appellant, and who was an orthodox minister according to law and "to the method of usage" of the Presbyterians was on the 17th day of May, 1732, duly settled and ordained to preach God's word to the inhabitants of Kingston. He became entitled to enter into and take possession of the land and enjoy it so that he might have the income and profits from it during the continuance and performance of the ministerial office just as his predecessor Miles had done before him. But George Mumford had gained possession of the land and refused to give it up and the appellant brought an action of trespass and ejectment in the inferior court of common pleas. On the last Tuesday in June, 1732, a verdict was found in favor of Mumford from which an appeal was taken to the superior court, and in turn to the King in Council.

The superior court had stated that the question was one of orthodoxy and that if the petitioner was an orthodox minister according to law, the land sued for would go to him. The court decided that the petitioner was not an orthodox minister according to law and therefore confirmed the judgment of the inferior court in favor of Mumford and condemned the petitioner to pay the costs. At this time, however, four of the judges who tried the case dissented from the rest and entered their dissent in due form. The case was heard before the committee of the Privy Council who reported July 16, 1734, that the judgments of the colonial courts should be reversed and the appellant,

Torrey, placed in possession of the land in question.[1] This was done by an order in council of July 18, 1734.[2]

The same parcel of land and the deliberation over the question of the meaning of the word orthodox reappears in 1736 in the appeal of James McSparran against Robert Hassard, a tenant of the Joseph Torrey of the earlier case for the recovery of the 280 acres of land.[3] The appeal was admitted January 26, 1737, and the security advanced by McSparran and a Thomas Sanford, a merchant of London, in February.[4] The case was heard before the committee and returned to the courts of Rhode Island to be determined on its merits.[5] It was brought on appeal for the second time by McSparran, March 8, 1740. The committee ordered the case to be heard May 8, 1741. But the final decision was not given by the committee until May 7, 1752, eleven years later.[6] The matter was heard at great length before the committee, the respondent being represented by Ryder and A. Hume Campbell, solicitors.

The statement of the case showed that by the second law passed in Rhode Island after the charter of 1663 it had been enacted "that all men professing Christianity and of competent estates and civil conversation who acknowledge and are obedient to the Civil Magistrate though of different judgments in religious affairs (Roman Catholics excepted) shall be admitted freemen and shall have the liberty to choose and be chosen officers in the colony both military and civil." This established the fact that no particular sect was meant by the word "orthodox" in Rhode Island. The original deed for the land in question

[1] *P. C. 2*, no. 93, pp. 527-9.

[2] *Ibid.*, p. 537; *Acts Privy Council*, vol. iii, p. 404.

[3] *P. C. 2*, no. 94, p. 24.

[4] *Acts Privy Council*, vol. iii, p. 390.

[5] *Ibid.*, p. 529.

[6] *Ibid.*, p. 530.

of three hundred acres was given by the original purchasers to one John Porter in exchange for his encouragement to preach God's word to the inhabitants of Kingston under the statement that the land was to go to "an orthodox person that shall be ordained to preach God's word".

In October, 1674, the land described was incorporated into a township known as King's Town by the legislature of the colony. Of the three hundred acres of land, twenty acres were occupied by Mr. Henry Gardner, and 280 acres by Mr. James Bundy. Mr. Samuel Niles came and preached for a while and tried to get possession of the tract of land held by Bundy. December 7, 1713, the town council of King's Town enacted that the farm of three hundred acres of land laid out and given by the Petequamscut purchasers for the ministry should be put to use and that the town council of the town should be empowered to let out the said land "to him or them until such time that a minister do appear to accept the same."

In 1715 eight persons wrote a letter from King's Town to the Secretary of the Society for the Propagation of the Gospel in Foreign Parts asking for a permanent ministry for King's Town. In 1716 fourteen persons again wrote asking for a permanent ministry. James Bundy transferred his house and right of possession to the 280 of the 300 acres in King's Town, January 12, 1719, to George Mumford for one hundred pounds. Another letter was written in 1720 by citizens of King's Town asking for a permanent ministry and the Society for the Propagation of the Gospel named the appellant, the Reverend James McSparran, a clergyman of the Church of England, who became by appointment of the Bishop of London permanent minister in Narragansett and thus, according to his petition, the rightful possessor of the land in question.[1]

[1] Hardwicke Papers, *British Museum Additional MSS.*, no. 36217, folio 44.

Mr. Gardner gave up the twenty acres but George Mumford, a dissenter, refused to deliver the possession of the 280 acres. A writ of ejectment was taken out by McSparran against Mumford. The original deed of 1668 was in the hands of one Jahleel Brenton, a dissenter, who would not give it up, so that the appellant could not set forth the original grant from the proprietors, but founded his declaration against Mumford upon the original purchaser's confirmation by the deed of 1679 and the survey of 1692, both of which were on record. The survey used the word "ministry" without a modifying word to express an "orthodox" minister.[1] To this Mumford entered a plea of abatement.

In 1724 the inferior and superior courts found judgment for Mumford with power to recover his costs. Thus the matter rested eight years, Mumford continuing possession and Brenton keeping the original grant. There was no one ordained minister of any sect of dissenters until May, 1732. This was when Joseph Torrey, a Presbyterian, came to preach in King's Town. The Torrey case as previously cited then came up and in July, 1734, the case coming on appeal, the King in Council put Torrey in possession of the land.[2] Torrey having recovered 280 acres of the three hundred brought suit for the recovery of the other twenty. This was decided against him and he transferred his right to the 280 acres to six persons as trustees for himself and others in the ministry and these trustees transferred the

[1] "And as the constant tradition was that Jahleel Brenton, Esq., a dissenter had the custody of that deed or original grant from the Proprietors, the appellant caused the most civil application to be made to him by a near relation of Mr. Brenton to produce that deed; but he thought fit to deny he had it though at the time he produced and showed it, this very deed in his own custody as is most indisputably proved." Hardwicke Papers, *Additional MSS.*, folio 44, no. 36217.

[2] *Ibid.*

property to Hassard who became the respondent in the case under discussion. In 1735 McSparran took out a capias in ejectment against Hassard and declared himself to have been an orthodox minister since 1721. The pleas of Hassard were overruled in the inferior courts and the case came on for trial before the superior court in 1739. The jury of this court awarded a verdict to the defendant and decreed that the plantiff should have his costs taxed at 19 pounds, 12 shillings, 10 pence. This was the case which was now before the Council for final determination.[1]

The respondent through his solicitors entered an able defense. He stated that Rhode Island had been settled by people who dissented from the discipline and church government of the Church of England. The tract purchased from the Indians in the Narragansett country had been bought by settlers, all of whom had been Presbyterians or of Congregational persuasion. That the religious sentiments of the first settlers in Rhode Island were not of Episcopal or Church of England persuasion was shown by the fact that the commissioners appointed by the king in 1665 ordered the baptism of children. As there was no minister of the Church of England at that time in the colony, these settlers must be Presbyterians, for none of the English churches but the established and Presbyterians received infants to baptism. The early proprietors who originally came to Massachusetts and thence to Rhode Island came for the express purpose of escaping the Church of England ceremony and the 300 acres were, therefore, intended as a ministry farm for the use of a Congregational minister. At the time that Mr. Samuel Niles preached in King's Town the Reverend Mr. Bridge, a Church of England minister, preached in the north part of

[1] Hardwicke Papers, *British Museum Additional MSS.*, no. 36217, folios 45-46.

King's town without making any pretension to the land. The people voted at a quarterly meeting in 1713 that the town council should let out the farm until a minister should appear for the same. The farm was leased to Bundy, and it was agreed that Bundy should have possession for four years, paying four pounds, at the end of which time the land should be redelivered to Niles or such other minister as had been appointed. Bundy executed a bond of one hundred pounds penalty under this agreement. By virtue of this Bundy kept possession until January 12, 1719, when he sold his interest to George Mumford, a son of one of the proprietors who had put Niles in possession in 1702. McSparran set up a Church of England society in 1721 and brought an action against Mumford.

The reasons why the case should be decided in the respondent's favor were then set forth. It very evidently appeared, according to the argument of the solicitors, that the lands in question were given for the use and support of a Presbyterian ministry; for although neither the vote of 1668 or the allotment of 1679 did in terms call it a Presbyterian ministry, yet the circumstances of the case necessarily required such a construction. It was absurd to imagine that Presbyterians would give part of their estate for a form of worship contrary to their own, and it was impossible they could mean a Church of England ministry, which was not introduced till many years after. The merits of the question had been heard twice in the most solemn manner and both determinations were grounded upon the point as to whether the lands were intended for the use of a Presbyterian or Episcopal minister. It was contended that this case was practically the same as the Torrey case and based upon the same question, the former case differing from the present only in the name of the parties. If the people of the colonies were to be indulged in bringing the same question before the king as often as they pleased, the determination of the crown could never be final. Also the determination of His Majesty in Council would in this way be subject to the review of the courts below in the colonies.

It was also stated that as to the argument that the original deed was left in the hands of Mr. Brenton who unjustly kept it in his custody and denied having it, this very objection carried the strongest evidence with it that this land was originally intended for the use of a Presbyterian minister. This was merely a vote of the proprietors for the laying out of the tract and although the appellant did not produce this at the trial yet it nowhere was proved that it was concealed by Brenton. The appellant did produce the argument of 1679 confirming the tract of land to and for the use of the ministry and also the deed of 1692 which made out as strong a title for him as if the original vote had been produced. This plainly showed, it was argued, that the final judgment of the colonial court was grounded on the evidence that the lands were given and intended for the use and support of a Presbyterian ministry.

When the case was heard at the Cockpit, Whitehall, in 1752 the committee decided that the whole matter was one involving the meaning of the word "orthodox" and decided in favor of the dissenter. Therefore, the judgment of the superior court was affirmed. The whole case illustrates vividly the attempt of the Privy Council to arrive at a fair and just decision, independent of prejudice. The committee were agreed that the meaning of the word would have given it to a Church of England minister, if the circumstances had not shown that this was not intended by the original purchasers.[1]

[1] On the outside of the printed matter prepared for this case appears in what is probably Yorke's own handwriting "Affirmed the sentence in favor of a dissenter. It seems agreed that the word should give it to

As an example of the non-enforcement of the decisions of the King in Council we may take the case of Leighton *vs* Frost which came on appeal from Massachusetts Bay in 1735. The case involved a disagreement between William Leighton of Kittery, who was employed to fell trees for the use of the royal navy, and John Frost, who complained that trees on his own private land had been used by Leighton. The appeal was brought by Leighton against two decisions in favor of Frost and asked that in any similar suits against Ralph Gulston, his agents or his workmen, appeals might be allowed though the sum should be less than three hundred pounds.

Leighton's petition, which was heard before the committee, stated that on June 19, 1730, permission had been given by the king to Ralph Gulston of the city of London, with his agents and workmen, to search the woods in Maine and New England and provide timber for the royal navy. Leighton, as a workman of Gulston, entered a tract of land, which was part of the province of Maine and did not belong to any private persons at the time that the license had been given for felling the trees, and cut down several trees. On the fourth of March, 1733, John Frost of Berwick in the county of York sued out a writ of attachment against the petitioner and also against one Ephraim Joy, commanding the sheriff of the county of York to attach the goods or estate of the petitioner and Ephraim Joy for the value of two hundred pounds or in want thereof to arrest them and take them to York. They were accused of having cut down trees in direct violation of an act of the assembly of Massachusetts Bay to prevent trespass. The sheriff attached a horse and other things of

a church of England minister . . . if other circumstances had not shown a contrary intent in ye donors." Hardwicke Papers, *British Museum Additional MSS.*, no. 36217, folio 44.

the petitioner and left a summons for him to appear at the return of the writ. Leighton acknowledged that he had entered in the tract mentioned but that it was as a workman of Gulston under the license granted by the crown and that only trees of dimensions specified had been taken.

The case was tried in the inferior court in April, 1734, which decided against Leighton to the amount of 121 pounds damages and costs of forty shillings. Leighton then appealed to the superior court. In June 1734 the judgment of the inferior court was affirmed. The case was then taken on appeal to the Privy Council where Leighton asked that the judgments might be reversed and the sum of money restored to him. This board recommended that the judgments be reversed, and the money restored, and a new trial should be given in the Massachusetts courts at which Leighton should plead not guilty and give any special matter in evidence which should be taken in writing and recorded with the verdict and an appeal allowed to the king in Council. This was ordered in April, 1735.[1]

In December, 1738, Leighton again petitioned the Council complaining that the governor, council and superior court of Massachusetts Bay had refused to carry into execution the order in council of April 29, 1736.[2] Before the committee the following February it was shown that the attorney for Leighton had produced the order of the council of April, 1736, before the superior court of Massachusetts where it was publicly read and ordered to be recorded but that consideration was postponed until June, 1737. At this time Leighton's attorney, by written motion, moved the

[1] Leighton *v.* Frost, *Acts Privy Council*, vol. iii, no. 345, pp. 461-470; Davis—A McF.—The case of Frost *v.* Leighton, *American Historical Review*, vol. ii, pp. 229-240. Schlesinger, "Colonial Appeals to the Privy Council," *Political Science Quarterly*, vol. xxviii, pp. 434-437.

[2] *Acts Privy Council*, vol. iii, p. 466.

court to award execution against Frost, but the superior court replied that the subject matter was such as required the most mature consideration and that the court would take it under consideration. This postponed the matter until June, 1738. Then the court declared that having considered "the Royal Charter together with the laws of the province and the constant usage and practice of the Court" the judges were of the opinion that they had no authority to give an order for such an execution.

Leighton then stated that the superior court had taken two years to consider whether it would obey the order in council and at length had stated that it could not pay any attention to it. Therefore, he applied to Governor Belcher setting forth the facts in the case and asking execution of the order. Belcher laid this before his council, and that body returned the opinion that they had no authority to give an order for the execution and Belcher wrote at the foot of the petition that, the advice of the council being agreeable to him, he was prevented from being of any service in the affair. The committee recommended and the Privy Council directed, March 22, 1739, that John Frost immediately restore to Leighton the money paid by him for damages and costs and that, in case he refused to comply, the superior court of the province should take the necessary steps to compel him to do so. The inferior court was required to pay due obedience to the orders of the Council and, that nothing might be wanting to carry the king's commands into execution, the king was requested to order and require the governor of the province to support the royal authority and to cause "every particular herein contained to be without delay duly and punctually complyed with." [1]

In 1743 David Dunbar, surveyor general of the king's

[1] *Acts Privy Council*, vol. iii, pp. 468-469.

woods in North America, set forth in a memorial to the home government that the order in favor of Leighton had not been complied with and asked that the present governor be requested to put the order in council in force because it would "have so good an effect as to deter others from attempts of the like kind". In June of the same year the clerk of the council wrote the governor of the province of Massachusetts Bay relating to the enforcement of the order saying that in case the order in council had not already been carried into execution, that this should be done at once, that a copy of the account of the proceedings should be sent to His Majesty in Council and in case the order had not been already carried into execution an account was to be transmitted to the Privy Council.

The case illustrates the obstruction that might be placed in the way of the execution of colonial law by the courts of the provinces. On the other hand, it shows clearly the neglect on the part of the home government which permitted one of its decrees to be treated so lightly. If the government of Massachusetts Bay could set at nought a judicial enactment of the King in Council it goes far toward explaining that feeling which Burke was later to call "the fierce spirit of liberty". That Massachusetts felt free to explain her position to the home government shows her growing independent attitude. It is also quite evident that the home government for various reasons was unable to deal successfully with this attitude.

The appeals reaching the King in Council in the early eighteenth century reflect the conditions of a developing community. More than that, they show the attempt of the English government to give to this developing community a legal system modelled and patterned after the one which it had so successfully developed. Complaints against the judicial methods employed in the colonial courts or against miscarriage of justice in the colonies met with the response that those methods must conform with the traditional English system. In addition, the appeals of this period show an attempt to understand and solve the intricate legal problems arising in the provinces. The precedent is established of having mercantile accounts submitted to a committee of merchants for arbitration, in order that a fair decision may be reached. In religious matters a dissenting minister received justice over the appeal of a Church of England divine. With the intricate land questions arising in the dependencies the home government was at times in difficulty but an attempt was made to settle these questions as impartially as possible, using the English land system as the basis for judgment. It is not surprising to find that, despite some opposition, a tremendous amount of respect had developed in the colonies, even this early, for the imperial system.

CHAPTER IV

Appeals to the King in Council

1745-1776

The appeals to the King in Council in this second period show the complex conditions of life which had developed in the American dependencies. The interest now lies in the reflection which the appeals throw upon colonial customs and thought as well as upon the imperial attitude toward the control over judicial matters in the colonies. The judicial machinery is well understood in the provinces and is respected even in those colonies which, feeling the development of an independent spirit, wished to oppose the prerogative of the home government. In the early years of this period the appeals are more numerous than they have been previously, showing that advantage is being taken of the privilege of appeal with the growth and development of the colonies. As the revolutionary years are approached, however, the appeals tend to become less and less frequent although the Council referred to the committee a petition for an appeal from a citizen of Charleston, South Carolina, as late as 1782.[1]

Among the cases important enough to deserve special attention are those arising over matters of finance, particularly over the depreciation of the issues of paper currency in the New England colonies. The rate of exchange varied from year to year between England and most of

[1] *Acts Privy Council*, vol. v, no. 420, p. 519.

the colonies. And when paper money was issued by one of the colonies the exchange differed not only between the various colonies but also within the same colony between the different issues. The only judicial redress in this financial confusion was by appeal to the King in Council in the hope that the home government might be able to make an adjustment which would give some sort of stability to the confused financial situation.

In November 1759 Thomas Deering of Boston, the executor of Henry Deering, petitioned for the hearing of his appeal from the judgment of the superior court of New Hampshire in 1758 in an action against Thomas Packer of Portsmouth, New Hampshire, for the payment of a debt of 2460 pounds and six per cent interest.[1] The case arose over the depreciation of the many issues of paper money in New England. From April, 1744, until April, 1750, Thomas Packer made several payments upon account in his indebtedness to Deering amounting to 3110 pounds in the old tenor bills. There was still due 2123 pounds, 14 shillings, 5 pence in 1750 at the time of the death of Henry Deering. Thomas Packer then offered in February 1751 some paper bills on the credit of New Hampshire which he alleged to be of 2000 pounds value and some bills on the credit of the colony of Connecticut which he valued at 200 pounds. Thomas Deering, who was the executor of the estate, objected to these, stating that the debt was payable in lawful money of New England or "good publick bills of Massachusetts" unless an allowance were made for the difference between the value of the bills tendered and the current lawful money in Massachusetts bills. In November, 1757, Deering brought suit against Packer for 4920 pounds in the inferior court of common pleas in

[1] *Acts Privy Council*, vol. iv, no. 407, p. 433.

New Hampshire and received a verdict for the amount. Packer moved to be heard in chancery. This was granted and he pleaded that tender had been made in February 1751 and insisted that interest ought to stop at that time. This the court allowed. On appeal, the superior court gave the same judgment and Deering then obtained a review in the same superior court but without a change in the final judgment. The case was heard before the committee which reported to the Council July 10, 1760. The next day the Council ordered that the judgments and verdicts be reversed and that the interest ought not to stop at the time tender was made. The debt should be considered cancelled when the respondent, Packer, paid to the appellant 1187 oz, 14 dwts, 20 grs. silver which was ascertained to be equal to the sum of 2,197 pounds, 7 shillings and 11 pence of the late old tenor bills of Massachusetts Bay, the computation to be made at the rate of thirty-seven shillings to the ounce of silver. In default of this payment within six months, the appellant could sue out execution upon the judgment together with five pounds sterling for costs.[1]

This case made a precedent upon which another appellant based his claim for justice with regard to the New England paper issues.[2] A London merchant, Barlow Trecothick, appealed in 1758 from the judgment in the previous year of the superior court of New Hampshire affirming two previous judgments in a suit for the recovery of 5770 pounds, 16 shillings in Massachusetts bills of credit of the old tenor. The appellant set forth the fact that the single question at issue upon his appeal was whether a British merchant selling his goods to a resident of the colonies should be paid about a quarter part of the

[1] *Acts Privy Council*, vol. iv, pp. 435-436; *British Museum Additional MSS.*, no. 36218, folio 44.

[2] *British Museum Additional MSS.*, no. 36218, folio 151.

original cost of the goods by being obliged to take the amount of the indebtedness in paper currency at the rate of exchange which governed at the time of the judgment or at the time of the appeal, when such paper currency had extremely depreciated. It was stated that it was an indisputable fact, that in all the colonies almost every individual merchant there was supported by his credit on his British merchant and if the situation with regard to the depreciation of paper currency should be legally tolerated a man so disposed would have nothing more to do than to buy in a vast quantity of goods and merchandise and delay the payment for two or three years when he need not pay half of its original cost if he could make use of the depreciating currency.

After stating the facts which showed Wentworth's indebtedness to Trecothick the whole question of the paper currency in New England was set forth. The four New England provinces had all issued their own respective paper money; this had circulated by common consent in each province. But in 1750, because of a stagnation of trade, the English Parliament passed an act in that year to restrain the issue of these paper currency bills.[1] Massachusetts actually called in and paid off her bills soon after, but the province of New Hampshire never made any provision for the payment of her bills, leaving them current and still depreciating, so that at the time of the appeal (1758) they were worth not more than thirty shillings currency for one shilling sterling.

The debt had been contracted in Massachusetts and was

[1] "An Act to regulate and restrain Paper Bills of Credit in his Majesty's Colonies or Plantations of Rhode Island and Providence Plantations, Connecticut, Massachusetts Bay and New Hampshire in America; and to prevent the same being legal tenders in Payments of Money."

to have been paid in Massachusetts money at a time when the appellant was resident at Boston, but as Wentworth was living in New Hampshire it became necessary to attempt to recover in the courts of New Hampshire. In these courts judgment was given to Trecothick in the new tenor bills of New Hampshire.[1] As the rate of exchange between New Hampshire and London at the time the debt was contracted and at the time the judgments had been given had varied from the rate of ten for one to an uncertain rate of probably 1 shilling, 19 pence to one, Trecothick objected. This amounted to only about one quarter part of the sum which the New Hampshire merchant acknowledged to be justly due and owing. The appellant objected to the judgments as attempts to deprive him of almost the whole of the debt due him and set forth his reasons for a favorable judgment from the King in Council.

These reasons were divided into three groups. First, that in as much as this was a debt for goods sold and delivered before and in the year 1749 when the exchange was in old tenor as ten shillings currency for one shilling sterling, or as had appeared previously in the case of Deering *vs.* Packer from this same colony of New Hampshire, the price of silver was at sixty shillings per ounce and as the rule governed in that case that the debt should be paid in silver, the same consideration was asked in this case, the appellant hoping to have the judgment rendered in sterling with interest. Second, it had been made clear that if the respondent were to prevail in the suit he would have kept the appellant, a British merchant, out of his money for eleven years and in the end not pay the half his indebtedness, to say nothing of

[1] *British Museum Additional MSS.*, no. 36218, folio 152. In the year 1742 a new issue of paper money was issued by the province of New Hampshire which was said to be more valuable than the former but which also had depreciated. It is from this that the distinction of bills of credit of the old tenor from bills of credit of the new tenor comes.

the interest. The paper money was still circulating and still depreciating in defiance of an act of the British Parliament to the contrary. Third, it had been proven that the money was to have been paid at Boston, where the debt was contracted, and since the bills of Massachusetts were always far better than those of New Hampshire it was from necessity only that the matter was brought into the New Hampshire courts and a judgment accepted involving the paper currency of that province.

The committee heard the case *ex parte,* no appearance having been entered for the respondent, and on April 5, 1762, the judgments of the New Hampshire courts were reversed and the respondent ordered to pay the appellant's costs.[1] The debt was judged to amount to 479 pounds, 9 shillings, 6 pence sterling and was to be paid in the silver currency of the province of Massachusetts or New Hampshire at the rate of five shillings sterling to the ounce of silver or fifty shillings Massachusetts currency which was the rate of the Massachusetts paper currency to silver in the year 1750.[2]

The King in Council was frequently called upon in this period to decide questions between the London merchant and the colonial. Here as in the previous period the facts in the cases would tend to show that the sympathy of the colonial courts was generally with the colonial planter and merchant. Not only was the decision given in his favor if the circumstances seemed to warrant, but the appeal to the King in Council was denied in many instances upon the ground that the amount involved was under value.

A single illustration will show the attitude in such cases. Two Bristol merchants, by name John Lidderdale and John

[1] *British Museum Additional MSS.*, no. 56218, folio 153.

[2] *Acts Privy Council,* vol. iv, no. 362, pp. 393-394.

Harmer, the surviving partners of Thomas Chamberlayne, deceased, brought a petition for an appeal February 25, 1755, from a judgment of the general court of Virginia in favor of John Chiswell, a merchant and planter of that province.[1] The appellant, Lidderdale, having been in the colonies for some time in the interests of his firm, resided in Virginia several years, where the respondent, Chiswell, met him and entered into business relations with him. At the death of Thomas Chamberlayne, Lidderdale and Harmer became the sole surviving members of the Bristol firm of Thomas Chamberlayne and Company. There was a correspondence between the appellants and the respondent as between planter and factor as to shipments of sugar consigned to the partnership house at Bristol. A letter of the respondent dated March 15, 1747, to the Bristol firm stated that 30 hgs. of tobacco had been sent on the ship *Virginian* and that it was agreed to send Lidderdale 100 hgs. more that season, but asked an advance of 400 or 500 pounds sterling on the tobacco of the year. Thereupon the appellants paid insurance and bills for Chiswell. The appellants notified Chiswell on August 29, 1748, that they had paid his insurance and bills. There was some further exchange of commodities and an extension of Chiswell's credit until it was found that the Bristol firm had exceeded their receipts by 233 pounds, 12 shillings and 3½ pence. The respondent made no further consignments and did not offer further to discharge his obligations but continued to 'draw' bills upon the two appelllants. The partners refused payment and the bills were protested. They brought an action in 1749 against the respondent upon the protested bills with interest and damages.

The respondent was able to delay the determination of

[1] *British Museum Additional MSS.*, no. 36217, folio 199. *Acts Privy Council*, vol. iv, no. 263.

this action for some four years but May 3, 1753, judgment was given for the Bristol merchants and Chiswell paid the amount of the judgment. The Bristol merchants now brought suit for the amount which Chiswell owed the firm under the act of Parliament for the more easy recovery of debts in the plantations.[1] The account was drawn up and adjusted to September 10, 1750. This was duly authenticated under the city seal of Bristol. In April 1751 action was brought in the general court of Virginia for the partnership debt with damages. The hearing was postponed by a series of half-yearly continuances from April 10, 1751, to April 10, 1754. Judgment was then given for Chiswell with costs. The appellants obtained permission to file a bill of exceptions. With this bill admitted, the Court gave judgment in favor of Chiswell with costs. The partners of the Bristol firm desired an appeal to the King but this was refused as being under value.[2] Then a petition was addressed to the Council and an order in council was issued by the lord justices dated June 24, 1755, admitting the appeal with the bill of exceptions included. On June 27 Hugh Hammersly, a solicitor of Lincoln's Inn, gave the required security for prosecuting the appeal. The case was heard before the committee on Monday, February 27, 1758.[3]

The appellants, through their solicitors, set forth the following argument. The action had been brought for an amount justly owing to the partnership on January 25, 1748, with interest from that time. All the agreements had been and should be reciprocal and if the appellants or either of them had agreed to pay the respondents bills there must

[1] 5 George II, ch. 7.

[2] The amount of the debt with the damages had been estimated by the Bristol firm at 400 pounds. *Additional MSS.*, no. 36217, folio 199.

[3] *Acts Privy Council*, vol. iv, p. 286.

have been an implied condition of their receiving adequate consignments. This was proved by the letters dated March 10, 1747 and August 29, 1748, in which it was shown that the appellant Lidderdale would not engage in the required advance without the concurrence of the partnership and that the respondent was not to draw for more than Lidderdale had agreed to, since it was stated that the merchants would be sorry if the bills had to be returned. It had been argued that the legislature provided the merchant an easy remedy for the recovery of his debts against the planter by the act in that regard. But should this present attempt prevail, the merchant must either continue to answer the demands of the planter to his own ruin or if he refused the bills of a planter, though without effects or consignments to answer the same, that refusal, by a jury and a bench of planters might be the means of depriving him of his return.[1]

The respondent Chiswell rested his case largely upon technicalities.[2] It was stated that the bill of exceptions had never been legally tendered until after the verdict and a day after the judgment had been given. The court of Virginia did nothing but what was legal and just in permitting the respondent to give evidence of the agreement by the letters. But the bill of exceptions and the evidence objected to "about which such a cloud is raised" seemed from the nature and circumstance of this case to be quite foreign to the case and out of all question. If the bill of exceptions were removed, the case would be reduced to a very brief point, namely, the plaintiff sued for a debt upon the defendant's assumption to pay the debt and the jury in a regular law court found the issue for the defendant by a

[1] *British Museum Additional MSS.*, no. 36217, folio 200.

[2] *Ibid.*, folio 203.

general verdict on the ground that the defendant did not assume the indebtedness. The appellants had shown that the only evidence which they could produce to the jury was their account and an affidavit to authenticate it. This affidavit was made in this case not as the Act of Parliament required it to be, but as an *ex parte* and extra-judicial affidavit made before this case began.

The committee reported its decision in the case to the Council and an order in council was issued April 1, 1758. By this the judgment of the Virginia court was reversed. The parties were then directed to a new trial, it having appeared that manifest injustice had been done the plaintiffs in the Virginia court. This declaration was made after due deliberation over the procedure in the colonial court particularly the permitting of the reading of the letter of August 1748 without proof.[1]

In 1759 the King in Council was called upon to pass upon the question of the status of negroes as property in the colonies in a case which came from Virginia. Lewis Burwell of the county of James City, Virginia, and Frances, his wife who was also one of the executors of the estate of James Bray, appealed from the decree of the general court of Virginia, given April 10, 1758, which had dismissed their bill against Carter Burwell, an executor of the estate of James Bray, and also against Elizabeth Johnson, and her husband Philip Johnson. This bill had been for the purpose of obtaining an account of the slaves belonging or due to be delivered to James Bray at his death.[2]

This appeal was occasioned by the fact that the appellants insisted that the courts of Virginia had put a wrong construction upon several of the acts of assembly of that

[1] Handwriting probably Yorke's on the outer cover of the statements of the solicitors. *Additional MSS.*, no. 36217.

[2] *Acts Privy Council*, vol. iv, p. 418.

colony on the question as to whether property in negroes was real, or whether they were real estate for particular purposes only. This in turn involved the question as to whether property in negroes could be entailed. Negroes and slaves were in their own nature and were taken to be in Virginia and in other of the British colonies chattels and personal estate until such time as by positive acts of the legislature, which had been passed in some but not all of the colonies, they had been declared to be real estate.[1]

James Bray had inherited from his grandfather some negroes as slaves, and he, dying, left his entire estate to his wife. The wife insisted that the negroes could not be entailed. This then involved two questions with regard to the property. First, whether the grandfather could entail his slaves and second, what power the grandson James Bray had over these slaves. These two questions involved an interpretation of two acts of the Virginia assembly.

The facts in the case were brought out in the hearings in the Virginia courts. It was insisted by the appellants that negroes never were in Virginia or in any other British colony declared by legislative act to be real estate with all the general properties and privileges of real estate in general, but only to be considered as real estate for such special and particular purposes as the several legislatures had enacted. The only Virginia act relative to these questions which had been passed prior to the bill and death of the gradfather, James Bray, was enacted in 1705. This declared slaves to be real estate but with a great number of clauses, provisos, and exceptions; and in the same clause which made them real estate it was in express terms enacted that they should descend according to the custom and manner of lands of inheritance in fee simple.[2] In 1727,

[1] *British Museum Additional MSS.*, no. 36218, folio 138a.

[2] An act declaring the negro, mulatto, and Indian slaves within the Dominion to be real estate. *Ibid.*, folio 138b.

after the death of the grandfather, James Bray, and the disposition of his estate by will, a new act was passed in Virginia to explain and amend the previous act of 1705. This new act provided that slaves might be annexed thereafter by their owners to entailed lands. In 1744 the grandson possessed of his share of his grandfather's lands and slaves died without issue and left all his property to his wife Frances Bray, who later married Lewis Burwell. An agreement was reached between the wife Frances and another member of the family, Thomas Bray, concerning the entailed lands and property by which Thomas Bray became possessed of some of the slaves belonging to James Bray. These slaves passed into the hands of Elizabeth Johnson, the daughter and heiress of Thomas Bray, and her husband Philip Johnson. The matter came up for hearing in 1758 on a bill of the plaintiffs, Frances and Lewis Burwell, for an accounting by Elizabeth and Philip Johnson of their property in slaves. The Virginia court ordered that the bill be dismissed and that the plaintiffs should pay the defendants the costs expended by them in the suit. From this decree the plaintiffs appealed to the King in Council.[1]

The case was heard before the Committee on March 16, 1762.[2] Learned counsel represented both sides, Pratt and Charles Yorke for the appellants and De Grey and Forester for the respondents.

The appellants stated their case as follows. Although by the act of 1705 negroes were declared to be real estate, they were made so only for particular purposes. It would be hard to allow of entails of negroes by implication upon that law, because when once created they can not be barred by any method established in the colony. James Bray, the

[1] *Additional MSS.*, no. 36218, folio 141.

[2] *Acts Privy Council*, vol. iv, p. 418.

grandson, was tenant in tail of the negroes by virtue of the will of his grandfather made in 1725. The act of the assembly, which made them entailable as annexed to lands entailed, was not passed until 1727, two years after the will was made. The act enabled the making of such entails only for the time to come. Therefore, deeds and devises limiting an estate tail in negroes antecedent to that law must be construed as vesting the whole ownership, on which no remainder could be limited unless it be restrained to take effect within a particular time or within the compass of a life or lives in being, as in personal property, or as of estates granted or devised in fee on which a remainder in fee can not be limited. The decree of the colonial court was extraordinary in dismissing the bill with costs when there was an admission and some proof also that James Bray, the grandson, had other negroes which came from his wife and her father, and the decree was wrong in not decreeing those negroes to the appellants and in not making inquiry into the property. The solicitors concluded by asking that the decree be reversed.[1]

The respondents stated their case in answer to this in the following argument. By the act of the assembly passed in Virginia in 1705 which was in full force at the time that James Bray the grandfather made his will the slaves were to be taken and adjudged to be real estate and not chattels. These were to descend to the heir as lands of inheritance would do. There could be no doubt that under this act slaves could be disposed of or devised by deed or will in the same manner as any real estate and consequently could be entailed. The words of the will were indisputably

[1] *British Museum Additional MSS.*, no. 36218, folio 142. Another appeal involving a question of property in slaves was that of Thomas and John Edmundson of Virginia *v.* William, Martha and Humphry Tabb, 1760. *Acts Privy Council*, vol. iv, p. 443.

sufficient to create a good estate tail in James Bray with remainder over to Thomas Bray. The subsequent act of 1727 did not, as it had been conceived, affect the case *ex post facto,* for the intent of this act was manifestly only to create a distinction where slaves were disposed of by themselves and where they were disposed of with lands. By this it was enacted that it should be lawful by deed or will where any lands should be settled in fee tail or otherwise to settle or devise slaves to go as part of the feehold which would lawfully annex them thereto and that they should go in possession or remainder with such lands. Where lands should be settled or devised in fee tail or otherwise, and in the same deed or will any slaves should be devised with the same limitations, the slaves should go therewith. This being the case under discussion, the respondents stated that this second act could never be construed to defeat the devise in this case but on the contrary confirmed and established it.[1]

The committee agreed with this argument and in its report to the Council March 16, 1762, recommended a judgment in favor of respondents. The Council affirmed the decree of the colonial court April 5, 1762.[2]

An attempt to bring out the irregularities to be found in the Massachusetts courts was made by the appeal of William Vassall in a case involving the question of defamation of character.[3] One William Fletcher, a citizen of Massachu-

[1] *Acts Privy Council,* folio 143.

[2] *Acts Privy Council,* vol. iv, no. 388.

[3] *Acts Privy Council,* vol. iv, no. 220. Another appeal involving defamation of character in this period was that of Charles Knowles, Rear Admiral of the White Squadron, from judgments of the courts at Boston in his action against Dr. William Douglas of that city for 10,000 pounds damages for "a scandalous and infamous libel" published in June, 1748. On January 5, 1749 the inferior court found for Douglas. On Knowles' appeal the superior court in February 1749

setts, brought an action in the inferior court of common pleas held in Boston charging William Vassall, gentleman, with having uttered words to the prejudice of his character. These were to the effect that Fletcher was not financially sound and that having purchased a ship he had insured it for more than it was worth and cast it away in order to cheat the people insuring it. Fletcher maintained that these statements had caused him to suffer greatly in his business and in respect to his good name. He had Vassall arrested who was held by the colonial authorities in what Vassall maintained was excessive bail. In the hearing of the case in the inferior court of common pleas Vassall made three several pleas. First, that the words charged as spoken could not be held to have been spoken within the jurisdiction of the court which was an inferior court created by an act of assembly to try civil actions; secondly, he pleaded the abatement of the writ for several defects therein and third, the plea of not guilty. The case was brought to trial and decided in favor of Vassall by this inferior court. Thereupon Vassall entered a special exception of record. Without producing witnesses or evidence of any sort Fletcher brought his action to trial before a jury and the verdict was again given for Vassall.

Fletcher now took advantage of an act of assembly which provided for writs of review and brought a writ of review March 18, 1752.[1] Vassall was again arrested and held to bail which he claimed was excessive since he had two judgments in his favor. The trial on the review occurred December 7, 1752. Here Fletcher introduced evidence and despite a statute of limitations of actions testimony was

awarded him 750 pounds and costs. Both parties brought a writ of review and on August 15, 1749, judgment was given in favor of Douglas with costs of court in each action. *Acts Privy Council*, vol. iv, no. 136, p. 107.

[1] 13, William III, ch. 16.

brought concerning statements made two years before the action was brought. The verdict was given against Vassall with the heavy damages of 2000 pounds of the province, amounting to 1500 pounds sterling. The jury, it was thought, was influenced by an irregularity of evidence and influence that was used against Vassall. Therefore Vassall was allowed an appeal to the King in Council, but was obliged to pay the sum of the damages because the court refused to stay the execution.[1]

In the hearing before the committee January 22, 1754, the appellant asked a reversal of the judgment. He argued that the colonial court should have passed on the pleas in abatement and the respondent should have replied to the appellant's plea of not guilty. Until this was done, it was maintained, the case could not be brought to a trial by jury and for this alone the verdict against Vassall and the judgment thereon were erroneous and ought to be set aside. He also stated that the trial in the inferior court should be a real trial and not a mock one and Fletcher produced no evidence until the trial by a writ of review. The damages were given for all the words in the action, and at the several times they were sworn to have been spoken by the appellant, and part of them were claimed to have been spoken more than two years before the action was brought and these were not actionable by act of the assembly. The damages being entire and not severable, it appeared upon the face of the record that they were given *inter alia* for words on which no action lay and consequently must be set aside. A great part of the evidence on which the verdict was founded was illegal and improper. The giving of such damages in New England as 1500 pounds sterling for words whence little or no damage really happened was most exorbitant. This sum had never before

[1] *British Museum Additional MSS.*, no. 36217, folio 46.

been given in this kind of action in any of the British plantations and would be considered very unusual even in the kingdom itself, as appeared from several actions tried in the city of London where "credit is much more delicate than in the Plantations". If this verdict be permitted to stand it must produce "an infinite number of these actions as a short and easy method of making a fortune, at the expense and ruin of many honest though perhaps rash and inconsiderate men". Furthermore, partiality was charged on the part of the Massachusetts court because the appellant was refused the right of cross-examining or putting such questions to the respondent and the witnesses as he wished, which was illegal and oppressive.

William Fletcher, the respondent, a merchant of great trade in Boston and a member of the assembly in that province, was brilliantly represented before the committee by the solicitors A. Hume Campbell and Charles Yorke. Here it was maintained that Vassall had conceived a dislike for Fletcher because of some lottery tickets in which both had been concerned. The arguments advanced for the respondent were; that the words in the declaration were actionable; that they had been spoken and repeated often against a merchant; that they were proven in the fullest manner and imported the greatest damage to the respondent's credit and reputation as a trader. Furthermore, the damages had been assessed by a jury acquainted with the circumstances of both parties and as no application was ever made to the court in the colony to set aside the verdict on account of the damages being considered excessive, they could not be deemed so in England.[1]

In accordance with the committee report of January 22, 1754, the judgment of the colonial court of review was re-

[1] The appellants and respondent's case, Vassall *v.* Fletcher, *British Museum MSS.*, no. 32217.

versed but the plaintiff in the action, Fletcher, was to be at liberty, after repaying Vassall the damages and costs awarded with interest, to proceed with a new action in the inferior court. The grounds upon which the judgment was reversed was that the plaintiff gave no evidence in either of the former trials on which the case could with any propriety be reviewed by a jury and was not therefore entitled to a writ of review.[1]

Three New England appeals are of interest in showing the state of affairs in those colonies with regard to finance. Edward Fogg of Rhode Island owed a sum of money to William Harvey of Charleston, South Carolina. Harvey had been given judgments against Fogg in the inferior and superior courts of Rhode Island. While this appeal was pending the assembly of Rhode Island abolished the court, but passed an act May 22, 1744, that persons who had appeals in the court might take them to the King in Council. The commitee found that Fogg had only prayed the appeal for the sake of unjustly delaying the payment of the sum of money and had not in any way prosecuted his appeal, although the time for so doing had elapsed. Consequently, November 28, 1745, the appeal was dismissed.[2] Joseph Sherburne, May 31, 1750, one of the captains of the New Hampshire regiments, complained of the proceeding of Governor Wentworth in denying to do justice to the petitioner in regard to his pay as captain of the foot from June 30, 1746 to October 31, 1747, and prayed that the governor might be ordered to make the petitioner satisfaction for his loss of time and expenses in prosecuting this affair as it had been occasioned by the governor's unjustifiable proceedings.[3] Along the same lines Governor

[1] *Acts Privy Council*, vol. iv, p. 226.

[2] *Acts Privy Council*, vol. iv, no. 12, p. 10.

[3] *Ibid.*, no. 130, p. 100.

Shirley of Massachusetts appealed from the judgment of the superior court at Boston of September 5, 1749, on a writ of review in a case between him and Samuel Waldo in relation to several bills of exchange and bills of credit issued to Samuel Waldo for the pay of one of the American regiments.[1]

The appeals involving questions of disposal of land are still in evidence. These appeals are from cases of dispute arising between the resident of one colony and the resident of another; from cases involving boundary disputes between the colonies, principally between Massachusetts and New Hampshire; from cases involving entailed estates; from cases involving disputes over questions of disposal of land by will with actions of ejectment and trespass. At least one of these appeals again involves the question of the Indian lands. Decisions are approved which meet the requirements of English tradition and which attempt to correct any deviation from the accepted standard.

Daniel Parke, a resident of Virginia and at his death Governor of the Leeward Islands, in order to throw the burden of his debts wholly upon his Virginian and English estates, made a will in 1709 which gave all his estate in the Leeward Islands to Lucy, the daughter of Mrs. Catherine Chester, or if she died in infancy to her mother. After her death the estate was to go to a godson, Julius Caesar Parke. A condition of the bequest was that Lucy Chester and her husband and heirs should take the name of Parke and use the coat of arms of that family, which belonged to Essex. If Julius Caesar Parke had no heirs the estate was to pass to the heirs of Frances, his daughter by his wife Jane Parke, whom he had left in Virginia and who had married John Custis of that colony. If there were no heirs by this daughter the estate was to go to his second daughter in

[1] *Acts Privy Council*, vol. iv, no. 130, p. 99.

Virginia, Lucy Byrd, the wife of William Byrd. The name of Parke was always to be taken by the possessor of the estates.[1]

Lucy Chester married Thomas Dunbar in the Leeward Islands, who took the name of Parke and sought to have Colonel Parke's debts paid by Custis out of the Virginian and English estates. On the death of Thomas Dunbar Parke proceedings were continued by Charles Dunbar and other executors of the will of Thomas Dunbar Parke. On the death of John Custis in Virginia, Daniel Parke Custis was left his sole heir and executor. The case was heard in the Virginia courts and April 10, 1754, the Virginia chancery dismissed the bill of Charles Dunbar, who was by that time the only surviving acting executor of the will of Thomas Dunbar Parke, against Daniel Parke Custis, who was the possessor of the estates in Virginia. Charles Dunbar felt that the Virginia court had shown partiality to one of its own residents and appealed the case which was referred to the committee April 3, 1755.[2]

From the nature of the final decision and as an attempt to justify the Virginia judgment it is the respondent's case which is of interest. The case was heard in the Privy Council chambers on Friday June 24, 1757. The respondent was represented by Yorke and Pratt as solicitors. Here it was brought out that Colonel Parke had an entailed estate in Virginia left him by his father. He left Virginia and went to England where he also had property. He saw service in Flanders. Extracts of letters written March 17, 1702 and July 30, 1703, were offered to show his affection for his daughter Frances in Virginia and his desire to leave her a plentiful fortune. He had repeated

[1] Dunbar *v.* Custis. *Acts Privy Council*, vol. iv, pp. 288-289; *British Museum Additional MSS.*, no. 36217.

[2] *Acts Privy Council*, vol. iv, no. 270.

this at the time of her marriage to John Custis. An affidavit was introduced to show that Colonel Parke had told Commissary Blair in London that he intended giving his wife and daughter his estate in Virginia. Upon these facts the respondents based several reasons why the judgment of the Virginia courts should be affirmed. In this case, it was maintained that the original will was not produced, much less proved, in Virginia and the only evidence of its existence was a pretended copy taken from the registry of Antigua where the original was not to be found. It was contrary to the rules of law and equity to make a decree upon the foundation of a will to affect real and personal estate, unless it has been duly proven. Therefore the appellant could not be entitled to a decree against the estate and effects of the testator in Virginia. In like manner it was impossible for the appellant to entitle himself to a decree in respect to the assets in England. At the time of registering it in Antigua two witnesses on oath, *ex parte*, attested their own signatures and that of the testator without the least notice of the third witness whose name was pretended to be subscribed. It was no just and reasonable construction to presume that the testator wished to have all his debts paid from the Virginia and English estates when the estate in the Leeward Islands was three times more in value than all the rest of the property. The manifest general intent of the testator certainly was not to have his own daughter for whom he had great affection bear the burden of his debts while his whole estate in the Leeward Islands passed to an illegitimate child. The letters introduced as evidence amounted to an agreement to settle a fortune upon Frances in equity.[1]

[1] *British Museum Additional MSS.*, no. 36217, folios 165-168. Yorke's own handwriting on the outside of the printed case "Decree varied—cause to stand over and plaintiff at liberty to demand his bill by

The committee reported their decision June 24, 1757. Six days later, in accordance with this report, the decree of the Virginia court was reversed and the case was ordered to stand over for a want of parties. But the plantiffs were allowed to amend their bill by adding the proper parties.[1]

Also with regard to the disposal of property Rhode Island was accused of showing partiality to her own residents. The colony was accused of refusing an appeal upon the technical grounds that the controversy was not of the value of 150 pounds sterling and the appeal had not been requested within the one-year limit in a case involving a dispute over land within her territory.[2] This was the appeal of Daniel Stanton of Philadelphia from the judgment of the superior court of Rhode Island in October, 1749, in favor of Elias Thompson, reversing a judgment of the superior court of that province in March, 1748. The matter in controversy between them was a fifth part of six hundred acres of land in King's County, Rhode Island known as Cedar Swamp. It also involved the question of a purchase of land from the Indians.

One Robert Stanton had purchased from the Indians a tract of land called Misquamacuck sold to them by the Indian chief, Sosoa, and known as Sosoa's purchase. He had formed a small landed society for settling this land. In 1669 a tract of land was erected into a township by act of assembly and this township was called Westerly. In

adding proper parties." The answer of Custis in November 1753 had objected to the omission of the other executors and of Daniel, Elizabeth and Lucy, children of Thomas Dunbar Parke, as parties.

[1] *Acts Privy Council*, vol. iv, p. 289.

[2] *British Museum Additional MSS.*, no. 36218, folio 1. On the outside of the printed brief in Yorke's handwriting "Right of appeal denied by Rhode Island because the controversy was not of 150 pounds sterling and the appeal would have to take place one year from the third of October, 1749."

1682 by another act the Assembly confirmed the purchase made from the Indians because of the doubt expressed by some of the right of individuals to buy land. The appellant, Daniel Stanton, derived title from Robert Stanton, one of the original proprietors. The respondent Elias Thompson also had a share in the land through his father by a conveyance of the land by one Benajah Bushual, September 17, 1720. The tract of land was surveyed by the province surveyor and he laid out a tract of part cedar swamp and part upland of about 600 acres. This was recorded as being possessed by three Rhode Island men, one of them Elias Thompson, and the appellant Daniel Stanton, who lived in Pennsylvania. The appellant in January 1746 began an action for the partition of the land in the inferior court of common pleas in Rhode Island. Thompson here pleaded that Stanton was not tenant in common with him and therefore had no right to a division of Cedar Swamp. At the trial Stanton proved the case as he had stated it and Thompson answered that the title of the land was vested in the freeholders of the town. The verdict in this hearing was against Stanton and judgment was entered against him with costs.

An appeal was then taken to the superior court where the judgment of the inferior court was reversed and a judgment of partition awarded to Stanton with costs. A writ of review was brought by Thompson before the superior court and the trial upon this was heard October, 1749. The jury here gave a decision reversing the former judgment of the superior court. The appeal was asked for some time later but was refused by the colonial court. Then Stanton made a direct petition and upon the committee report of February 12, 1756, the appeal was admitted five days later and on the twenty-eighth of the month Richard Partridge gave the security for the hearing.[1]

[1] *Acts Privy Council*, vol. iv, p. 287, no. 266.

The case was heard before the committee of the Council March 2, 1759. The respondent pleaded that the deed of purchase from Sosoa was merely a surrender of his right to the lands and was not in its nature a conveyance or deed of sale of the lands in fee simple. The purchasers could not in the year 1660 accept a legal estate in fee simple in lands in Rhode Lsland, not having at that time any grant or license from the crown to make such a purchase. Allowing the most liberal contruction, an estate in joint-tenancy was created and this must either have continued or been severed. If it continued there was no basis for a demand of one fifth part and if it was severed it was impossible to determine Stanton's fifth part. Neither Robert Stanton, the original purchaser, himself, or any of his descendants ever contributed a penny to the improvement of the land or ever possessed one foot of the purchased land or ever directly or indirectly set up any claim to the land until the present case arose. Finally, it was argued that the laws of England antecedent to 1663, particularly in this case the statutes of limitation, of their own proper authority extended to Rhode Island. In addition, the acts of the assembly state that the laws and statutes of England should be in force there. By these laws a total lapse of eighty-six years had passed without any claims being made to the land. Moreover it was stated that the appellant by living in a different province had prevented the respondent from obtaining any payment of the costs given in the Rhode Island courts, but in addition had drawn the respondent into the expense of defending his appeal. The appeal was dismissed March 3, 1759.[1]

The difficulties occasioned by the settlement of the bound-

[1] Hardwicke Papers. *British Museum Additional MSS.*, no. 36218, folio 8. In the handwriting on the outside of the printed case "decree affirmed"; *Acts Privy Council*, vol. iv, p. 287.

ary disputes between Massachusetts and New Hampshire became the basis of a series of appeals to the King in Council. A Board of Trade representation upon the matter containing a statement of the difficulties and disputes which had arisen in New Hampshire with respect to the property in lands and which had affected the peace and development of the province was referred to the committee February 7, 1753.[1] This Board of Trade representation was read in March and again in July and decision in the matter ordered to be delayed until further information should be forthcoming from the colonies. The matter was brought to the notice of the committee again, however, by a second representation of the Board of Trade resulting from a petition of the Reverend Timothy Walker of New Hampshire on behalf of himself and other proprietors of lands in the colony. This petition set forth that by virtue of grants from the province of Massachusetts Bay, made more than twenty years before, he and other proprietors had become possessed of many small parcels of land which by the settlement of the boundary between Massachusetts and New Hampshire had been determined to lie within the province of New Hampshire. Actions of ejectment had been brought by persons pretending to have holdings of the same lands from the governor of New Hampshire. As several of the parcels of land were separately of a smaller value than that for which, by the king's instructions, an appeal was allowed to His Majesty in Council, the petitioner asked that the king should explain his intructions or give further instructions as might admit appeals to the Council, in cases where the matter in question related to titles in lands although the value of the lands immediately appealed for be less than allowed. The committee requested the Board of Trade, July

[1] *Acts Privy Council*, vol. iv, no. 202.

23, 1755, to prepare additional instructions and these were reported back by the committee on August 7. Five days later an order was issued recommending that the petition be granted as the attorney and solicitor general had considered it and found it convenient and reasonable.[1]

With regard to this question two appeals reached the King in Council. These were appeals from judgments in the New Hampshire courts in favor of the proprietors of the township of Bow in that province. The first of these was allowed in March, 1754, upon a petition of John Merrill.[2] The second was the appeal of Benjamin Rolfe and others in 1762 from two verdicts of the inferior and superior courts of New Hampshire in September and November, 1760.[3] The home government did what it could in a legal way in both these cases to straighten out the difficulties.

Merrill's appeal in 1754 set forth the facts in the case. In 1755 Benjamin Stephens and others had applied from the government of Massachusetts Bay for a grant of land at Pennycock and this had been granted by the council, assembly and governor. Agreeably to this the land was surveyed in 1726 and in February of the next year several settlers were admitted to the tract along the Merrimac of whom John Merrill was one. In 1733 the settlement had grown to such proportions that it was incorporated into a township by the name of Rumford by an act of the assembly of Massachusetts which was confirmed by the king. Later the king appointed a commission to determine the

[1] *Acts Privy Council*, vol. iv, pp. 197-198.

[2] Merrill *v.* Proprietors of the township of Bow. *Acts Privy Council*, vol. iv, no. 231, pp. 239-243.

[3] Benjamin Rolfe, Esq. *et al.* *v.* Proprietors of the Common and Undivided Lands lying within the township of Bow in the Province of New Hampshire. Hardwicke Papers, *British Museum Additional MSS.*, no. 36218, folio 181.

boundary between New Hampshire and Massachusetts when a dispute arose over the question, but with the express declaration that nothing was to be done by the commission which would affect private property. In 1740 an order in council gave the limits of the two colonies according to the decision of the commission appointed to determine the boundaries and by this Rumford which had been understood previously to be in Massachusetts was now placed in New Hampshire. On November 14, 1750, certain persons from New Hampshire, in the name of the proprietors of the common and undivided lands lying in and being in the town of Bow, brought an action of ejectment against John Merrill and others in the inferior court of common pleas held at Portsmouth by which they demanded of Merrill eight acres of land with the appurtenances. These New Hampshire people alleged that their title went back to 1727 and that Merrill had entered upon the land and had kept them from possession for the space of twenty-three years.

It was determined to make an issue of the case. Merrill pleaded not guilty on March 7, 1750, when the case came for hearing in the inferior court. The jury here gave a verdict for Merrill with costs of court. The plaintiffs appealed to the next superior court of judicature held in December, 1752. At this trial the plaintiffs produced a grant dated May 20, 1727, made by John Wentworth as lieutenant governor of New Hampshire for a tract of land to be a town incorporated under the name of Bow. The plaintiffs also produced a return of the laying out of the town of Bow in 1728 which interfered in a considerable manner with the town of Rumford. The plaintiffs also introduced oral evidence to show that objection had been made by them to the settlement at Rumford, although nothing definite was done until the boundary dispute was settled. The jury in this trial in the superior court gave their verdict for the plaintiffs; the former judgment was reversed with costs of court. Merrill brought a writ of review before the superior court and in August, 1753, this court affirmed the former judgment of the superior court and stated that Merrill should pay the costs which amounted to 18 pounds, 5 shillings.

Merrill asked for an appeal to the King in Council. This was denied by the superior court because the premises were not of sufficient value. He then petitioned the king for an appeal and this was granted. It was felt that the appeal should be granted because it involved a question affecting Merrill's right to several other lands of considerable value in the whole and much exceeding the sum limited by the royal instructions. This appeal also affected the rights of other persons who were placed in the same circumstances and who held land under the same title. The appeal therefore was granted to avoid a multiplicity of other suits of the same nature.[1] June 24, 1755, after a report from the committee who heard the case in May the judgments against Merrill were reversed and an order issued that he should have restored to him all he had lost by the judgments.[2]

Against the aggression of the proprietors of the township of Bow who claimed one thousand acres as part of their grant of eighty-one square miles from John Wentworth, governor of New Hampshire in 1727, the second appeal reached the King in Council in 1762. In August, 1728, several persons who had served as volunteers against the Indians under Captain John Lovewell prayed that a tract of land might be granted to them for their services in the war. This was granted by the house of representatives of Massachusetts and six miles square lying on each side of

[1] *Acts Privy Council*, vol. iv, p. 243.

[2] *Ibid.*, p. 239.

the Merrimac River and to begin where Rumford ended was given to the forty-seven soldiers who were with Captain Lovewell at Pigwackett. This grant was surveyed and confirmed to the new settlers July 9, 1729. These proprietors then carried on their settlement which adjoined that at Rumford and in 1737 had "a good parish filled with inhabitants". Of course, these settlements came into conflict with the New Hampshire proprietors of the township of Bow as soon as the boundary dispute was settled by the king's commission. The case was heard in the inferior and superior courts of New Hampshire which invariably returned a verdict for the citizens of the province. The case was heard before the committee on December 17, 1762. Two days later, basing decision upon the precedent established by the preceding case, the judgments were reversed and the appellants were restored to all that they had lost through these judgments.[1]

In three cases over control of tracts of land the King in Council based decisions on technicalities which were involved in the judgments of the colonial courts. Concerning the will of Henry Sherburne of New Hampshire, and his estate John Sherburne appealed from a judgment of the supreme court of probate of wills in 1758 in favor of the other children of the testator. In April, 1762, the judgment of the colonial court was reversed by the King in Council with the statement that the court of probate had no jurisdiction in so far as the will related to real estate, but upon the rest of the case the decision of 1758 might stand affirmed.[2] An appeal from Virginia concerning a decree

[1] *Acts Privy Council*, vol. iv, pp. 527-530. *British Museum Additional MSS.*, no. 36218, folios 181-192. Maps showing extension of the Rumford settlement, folio 192.

[2] *British Museum Additional MSS.*, no. 36218, folio 147. *Acts Privy Council*, vol. iv, no. 382.

made in the general court of chancery in April, 1761, relating to the payment of several legacies provided for by the will of Neil Buchanan brought a speedy and definite answer from the Council.[1] The decree of the chancery court, which, it was definitely stated, should not have been carried into execution pending the appeal, was reversed and the money received by the respondents was to be repaid with four per cent interest with the deduction of the dividend of seven shillings in the pound payable under the commission in respect to debts from the estate of a bankrupt. The appeal of John Potter of South Kingston, Rhode Island from the judgments of the inferior and superior courts in that province in 1761 in favor of George Hazard was dismissed with twenty pounds costs. Hazard had been a defendant to an action of trespass and ejectment brought by Potter to recover possession of Little Comfort Island in Point Judith Pond, South Kingston. The defense maintained that Potter's action was barred by twenty years' uninterrupted possession. This the Council upheld.[2]

In a Rhode Island case involving property in land with a dwelling house which had been mortgaged, the King in Council took exception to the judgments of the colonial court.[3] One Gideon Cornell mortgaged his house and land in Newport to Thomas Shearman in 1753 for the sum of 6000 pounds Rhode Island currency. The deed was executed by Cornell and Rebecca, his wife, and was recorded at Newport September 27, 1753. Later Shearman became

[1] Samuel Richards *et al. v.* John Judson *et al., British Museum Additional MSS.*, no. 36218, folio 199-204. The statement of the case is given with Lord Mansfield's reasons for reversing the decree of the court below. This case involved the act of the Virginia Assembly for the better recovering of debts due inhabitants.

[2] Potter *v.* Hazard. *Additional MSS.*, no. 36218, folio 240. *Acts Privy Council*, vol. iv, no. 489.

[3] *Acts Privy Council*, vol. iv, no. 603.

bound to Cornell in the sum of 13,200 pounds current passable bills of public credit, old tenor. By agreement this was to be void upon payment by Cornell to Shearman of the 6000 pounds on the twenty-first day of September, 1754. He was also to pay and discharge all obligations given by both of them to any persons whatsoever before the twenty-first day of September 1754. In return the property was to be re-conveyed by Shearman to Cornell. This bond from Shearman to Cornell was executed September 23, 1753. Shearman acknowledged this bond before a justice of the peace, but Cornell neglected to have it recorded as he should have done, according to a law of the colony passed in 1714.[1]

Gideon Cornell being in possession of the mortgaged premises let them to one Benjamin Nichols at 300 pounds currency per annum. On the twenty-first of September, 1754, the mortgage money not having been paid Shearman took possession of the property and received the 300 pounds for the first year's rent. He then let the house to Nichols for 200 pounds per annum and Nichols expended the sum of 29 pounds, 17 shillings, 10 pence in necessary repairs during his occupancy from 1754 to 1756. On the 13th of December, 1756, Shearman and his wife by deed conveyed the property to Joseph Wanton and this was recorded February, 1757. From the time of his purchase Wanton continued in quiet possession of the premises and expended sums in repairs amounting to 960 pounds, 4 shillings, 10 pence currency by which the property greatly increased in value. Cornell, finding the estate greatly improved and thinking he might recover the premises with the improvements upon the payment of the nominal sum borrowed by

[1] An Act entitled "An Act for Registering Deeds and Conveyances and for the preventing of clandestine and uncertain sale of Houses and Lands." *Additional MSS.*, no. 36220, folio 115.

him, nothwithstanding that the estate in law had become absolute and that the remedy should have been by a bill in equity, brought an action of trespass and ejectment in the inferior court of common pleas at Newport. The decision of this court in a trial held May 30, 1763, was that Cornell should recover the possession of the land upon the payment of 6600 pounds old tenor bills of credit, and one year's interest. Shearman appealed the case to the superior court. Here it was decided that Shearman's plea was insufficient to bar Cornell's action and that Cornell should recover the premises from Shearman if he should pay to Shearman the full sum of 363 pounds reckoned at the rate or six shillings to the Spanish dollar. From this decision an appeal was taken to the King in Council.[1]

The case was heard before the committee on June 10, 1767. Through his attorneys, Yorke and Forrester, the appellant stated that the sum adjudged to be paid was no equivalent for the sum borrowed in September, 1753. At the time the mortgage was made a Spanish milled dollar was equal in value to 3 pounds, 10 shillings of the bills borrowed; in the year 1763 when the ejectment was brought it was equal to 7 pounds of the same bills. No legal tender had been made because there was by the act of Parliament restraining paper bills of credit in His Majesty's colonies,[2] nothing therein contained to make any bills of credit in the colonies legal tender. The several sums laid out in repairs and improvements of the mortgaged premises ought to have been allowed. The whole amount justly due amounted to 961 pounds, 10 shillings, 4 pence in old tenor bills. On report of the committee the judgments of the colonial courts were reversed and Cornell was to recover the premises in dispute on condition of paying to Shearman within a time

[1] *Additional Mss.*, no. 36220, folio 115.

[2] 24 George III, ch. 53.

to be limited by the colonial court a sum of 18,087 pounds, 10 shillings, 4 pence with six per cent interest from May 21, 1763.[1]

It has been pointed out that merchants, because of the difficulties involved in the colonial trade, were often appellants from the decisions of the colonial courts. In the later eighteenth century the nature of these appeals become much more complex. They involve breach of contract, insurance and bottomry. In addition they call in question the right of commanders of the government ships to bring cargoes before courts of admiralty without cause. The difficulties of colonial shipping are shown in this group of appeals.

A case involving a question of breach of contract came on appeal from Pennsylvania in 1766.[2] Thomas Harper, John Nixon and Company, owners of a ship called *Molly* of two hundred tons burden by an indenture of charter party of affreightment October 29, 1759, let to John Long and William Plumstead the ship for a voyage to Porte-au-Prince. This was to be made upon certain terms and conditions. Thomas Harper, John Nixon and Company by the charter party covenanted that the ship should be provided for a voyage with all speed; should be loaded as the freighters should think fit and should sail with the first opportunity of wind and weather. The destination of the ship was to be Porte-au-Prince, if the unloading would be permitted by the Governor and proper officers. If not permitted to unload at Porte-au-Prince the ship was to sail directly to Monte Christo in Hispaniola and there deliver her outward bound cargo. At whatever port the ship stopped it was to remain seventy days and receive such freight as the agents and factors should have ready and return to

[1] *Acts Privy Council*, vol. iv, p. 718.

[2] *Acts Privy Council*, vol. iv, no. 639.

Philadelphia. To Thomas Harper, John Nixon and Company freight was to be paid at the rate of four pounds per hogshead Pennsylvania currency. If the ship should happen not to be fully loaded at these places dead freight was to be paid. The freighters were also to pay demurrage for as many days as the ship should happen to be detained over and above the limit of seventy days. The owners were to bear all expenses of the ship except the expense for a commission for a flag at Porte-au-Prince and for the permission to trade and unload and any extraordinary expenses out and back. The freighters were to have the liberty to load rum or cotton on the ship to fill up the cargo if it were paid for at the current and reasonable rate.

An action was brought by Thomas Harper, John Nixon and Company in the supreme court of the province of Pennsylvania against the appellants for a breach of covenant in the charter party of affreightment in the year 1760. Here it was stated that the ship *Molly* had sailed in November, 1759, reached Porte-au-Prince on the twentieth of the month and there loaded 120 barrels of sugar, 18 barrels of indigo, and two trunks of dry goods. The ship thus loaded was seized on the high seas by Frederick Maitland, commander of His Majesty's ship *Lively* and carried into Port Royal in the island of Jamaica where it was brought before the admiralty court as lawful prize. The court here decided that the ship could not be held and Maitland appealed the case to the Lord Commissioner of the High Court of Admiralty. The cargo was unloaded and appraised as required by law. It was then claimed that the cargo was turned over to Long and Plumstead and on express order from Harper, Nixon and Company the ship returned to Philadelphia without the cargo. The company also maintained that the freight had not been paid to them.[1]

[1] *British Museum Additional MSS.*, no. 36220, folio 105. John Long and William Plumstead *v.* Thomas Harper, John Nixon and Company.

The case was tried on October 9th, the Company maintaining that the merchants had not performed the covenants in the charter party as they maintained. The merchants demurred to the evidence offered as not sufficient in law and asked that the jurors be discharged. The company joined in the demurrer and asked that judgment be given. On the 25th of April, 1762, judgment was given by the court in favor of the company, stating that the merchants should pay damages and costs to the amount of 1616 pounds, 14 shillings, 10 pence. From this judgment the merchants appealed the case to the King in Council.[1]

The case was heard before the committee of the Privy Council in the council chamber at the Cockpit on June 10, 1767. The appellants were represented by the attorneys Perryn and Yorke and the respondents by William de Grey and Jackson. The appellants maintained that Maitland had unlawfully taken and detained the ship and her cargo and therefore that the respondents should have sought satisfaction from Maitland and not from the appellants. That the ship's arrival in Philadelphia and the delivery of the cargo had not been prevented by the appellants and consequently they were not liable. The respondents replied by stating that there was no reason for a new trial as the jury in the supreme court had found all the evidence and no more had been offered by the appellants. The judgment was well founded since the capture and restraint of the ship was in no manner owing to the neglect of the respondents but was due to Maitland's mistake of thinking the cargo French property; this was due to the destination of the ship's voyage which was at the disposal of the appellants. The captain of the ship was obliged by the express order of the appellants or their agents to proceed to Philadelphia

[1] *Ibid.*, folio 106-108.

without the cargo.[1] The committee reported in favor of the respondents and on June 26th the judgment of the supreme court of April 1765 was affirmed.[2]

A case somewhat similar involving a London merchant came from the courts of Rhode Island. Jacob Isaacs brought an action against William Stead, a merchant of London, in the inferior and superior courts at Newport in May, 1764, and March, 1765, concerning the insurance of the ship *Rising Sun.* Stead appealed the case and on March 11, 1769, both judgments were reversed and a new trial ordered. It appeared in the trial that Stead had failed to carry out the full directions given him by Isaacs for insuring the ship in London. Consequently, after its loss on the Mosquito Coast, Isaacs received no compensation as the policy taken out by Stead had plainly stated that it was for the voyage from Honduras to Europe. On the other hand, the Council held, that Isaacs had not proven the value of the cargo in the Rhode Island courts so that the jury had no foundation for estimating the damages as they had done in the colonial hearings.[3]

As an example of the appeals concerning religious difficulties one case from Virginia may be taken. One William Kay, clerk, was by the governor of Virginia and the commissary recommended to the vestry of the parish church of Lunenburg in Richmond County, to officiate as minister. He was received as the officiating minister and was permitted to live in the glebe house. On August 4, 1746, seven of the vestrymen gave Kay notice to depart and stated that they would pay him for the time he had worked among them. To this letter Kay gave no answer. Then the vestry ordered the church locked; in order that the glebe lands might re-

[1] *British Museum Additional Mss.*, no. 36220, folio 110.

[2] *Acts Privy Council*, vol. iv, no. 639.

[3] *Ibid.*, no. 649, p. 759.

main in the hands of the parish they put William Degge, George Russell and Thomas Russell into possession of these lands as tenants of the parish. William Kay brought an action of trespass in the general court of the colony against the tenants of the glebe. The case was tried twice upon the issue as to whether the reception of a minister under a Virginia statute of 1727 would enable him to maintain an action of trespass committed on glebe land without induction against persons acting under an order of the vestry. It was decided April 21, 1749, that Kay could recover from the tenants thirty pounds sterling with damages and costs. The case was appealed and was admitted October 31, 1751. Two London merchants gave the security for the prosecution of the case. The hearing occurred May 15, 1753, and the appeal was dismissed with 80 pounds sterling costs June sixth.[1]

No survey of eighteenth century appeals to the King in Council would be complete without mention of the cases concerning the dismissal of two of the instructional force of William and Mary College. These were the Reverend John Camm, professor of divinity, and the Reverend Richard Graham, professor of natural philosophy. Considering that they had been removed by the Rector, visitors and governors of William and Mary College without cause, they obtained writs of mandamus for their restoration unless good cause were shown at the next general court to be held at Williamsburg. A return was made to these writs on April 10, 1759, and the case was heard in October. At the trial Francis Fauquier, the lieutenant governor, and the other judges of the court ordered the writs to be quashed. The cases of both men were taken to the King in Council and heard before the committee on March 12, 1763, at the

[1] William Degge *et al. v.* William Kay, Clerk. *Acts Privy Council,* vol. iv, no. 145.

Cockpit, Whitehall. The college was represented by Yorke and Forrester as solicitors and the appellants by Norton and Willis.[1]

The appellants argued that as the affair had arisen over the dismissal of an usher, the president and six masters or professors had by the statutes an undoubted right to appoint such an usher as well as all officers necessary for the college business. Consequently, the appellants had done nothing wrong in dismissing the usher, as the power of dismissal was implied with the appointing power. The interposition of the visitors was required only in matters of great weight and consequence, when the president and the masters could not agree. It was further stated that no regular complaint was ever lodged against the appellants, no witnesses were examined and the removal was made upon common report and hearsay with no attempt made at all to give the appellants a chance to be heard. The appellants had refused to assign a reason for the removal of the usher, the exercise of a power which they undoubtedly had a right to exercise and which could not be deemed contumacious action or one justly subjecting them to censure. The appellants insisted upon the right of being heard after being duly summoned and "days given" them in which to appear and make a defense.

The respondents answered that the charter of the college expressly gave Francis Nicholson and his associates the power of appointing the visitors and investing them with the power of removing the president and professors and naming others in their place. The respondents further

[1] John Camm, Clerk *v.* Rector, Visitors and Governors of William and Mary College. *British Museum Additional MSS.*, no. 36218, folio 223. Richard Graham *v.* Rector, Visitors and Governors of William and Mary College. *British Museum Additional MSS.*, no. 36218, folio 227.

stated that they had wished to inquire into the matter of the removal of the usher, but were obstructed by the refusal of the appellants to give a reason upon the pretense of the idea that the usher was appointable and removable only by the president and masters. This was argued to be false in fact, for the statute gave them only the power of nominating but not of removing an usher. The refusal of the appellants to assign a reason for the removal of an usher was an evident contumacy and clearly a good cause of deprivation of position.[1] On March 16, 1763, the Council sustained both appeals.[2]

John Camm also figured in another appeal from a judgment of the general court at Williamsburg, Virginia over a question of the status of tobacco as legal currency in Virginia for clergymen.[3] By virtue of a statute of 1748 the clergymen of the established church were entitled to sixteen thousand pounds of tobacco as a yearly salary. In 1755 and again in 1758 because of the inter-colonial wars the assembly passed acts allowing all public dues in which would be included the salaries of the clergy to be paid either in kind or in money. The rate fixed was two pence for a pound of tobacco. By 1760 tobacco was worth considerably more, about six pence per pound, and the clergy were dissatisfied with the legislation of the colony. Upon the recommendation of the Bishop of London the Act of 1758 was vetoed by the king. Whereupon the clergy began suits to recover the unpaid portions of their salaries. This was one of the several cases begun by the clergy.

The Reverend John Camm petitioned February 6, 1765, for a day for hearing his appeal against the judgment of

[1] *British Museum Additional MSS.*, no. 36218, folios 225-226; folios 228, 229, 230.

[2] *Acts Privy Council*, vol. iv, p. 530, no. 473.

[3] *Ibid.*, no. 588, p. 699.

the Williamsburg court in favor of Charles Hansford, Jr., and William Moss, collectors of the Yorkhampton parish levy for 17,280 pounds of tobacco, as his salary for one year as minister of the parish of Yorkhampton. By the act of 1748 the appellant claimed that he was entitled to 16,000 pounds of tobacco as his yearly salary, with an allowance of four pounds per hundred for shrinkage. With this allowance the total was 17,280 pounds. By another Virginia act the sheriffs or other collectors of levies and fees should before the last day of May each year pay and deliver to each creditor according to their respective debts and claims. If any sheriff or collector should refuse or delay to make payment he should pay to the party aggrieved double the value of the tobacco so refused or delayed if the debt due exceeded the value of 200 pounds. Camm maintained that his yearly salary in tobacco with the shrinkage was worth 432 pounds current money of Virginia and with the penalty of the double value would be 864 pounds Virginia currency.[1]

The committee heard the case November 27th, the appellant being represented by solicitors Norton and Willis and the respondents by De Grey and Yorke.[2]

The appellant justified the suit under the act of 1748 and disregarded the subsequent acts of the Virginia legislature. It was set forth that every commission to a governor referred to his instructions, and consequently these instructions were incorporated with and made part of the commission. Therefore, every act of the council and the assembly without a suspending clause which repealed or altered an act confirmed by the crown was void. An act that had received the sanction of the crown can not be altered or repealed by a lesser authority. The council and assembly could not

[1] *British Museum Additional MSS.*, no. 36220, folios 52-53.

[2] *Acts Privy Council*, vol. iv, p. 699.

make an act such as that of 1758 repugnant to reason and fundamentally unjust. This was really the more audacious as the assembly in Virginia in 1753 had petitioned the king for permission to repeal and alter some laws which had been confirmed by the crown without a suspending clause. The order of March 7, 1753, especially forbade this. The act of 1758 which had provided for the payment of the salary in money or in kind had had its full mischievous effect before the order in council of August 10, 1739. Therefore, the order must have meant to declare the act void in itself *ab initio* or the order was nugatory and of no sort of effect.[1]

The respondent's case stated that the action was brought to recover a penalty under an act of assembly passed in the year 1748; but it could not be conceived that this action was maintained by force of this act of the assembly, independently of any consideration of the subsequent act of 1758, because it did not appear that the defendants had received any inspectors' notes in satisfaction of the plaintiff's debts or claims or that they refused to delay to make such payments. The act of 1748 did not seem to be applicable because the collectors were guilty of no fraud or embezzlement or of converting tobacco received on a public account to their own use, but acted in direct obedience to the law of 1758. If the penalty should be recovered against the defendants they would have incurred a penalty for doing what the laws of the country compelled them to do. The legal process did not seem to be quite consistent. If the collectors had neglected their duty or been guilty of a breach of trust in the execution of their office, the bond entered into by them for the faithful discharge of their office might mave been put in suit, which would have been the proper remedy. The governor with the advice and consent of the council and

[1] *British Museum Additional MSS.*, no. 36220, folio 54.

the general assembly had full power to make laws for the public good provided they were transmitted within three months' time to the crown for approbation or disallowance. The act of 1758 was, therefore, a good and valid law in Virginia until June 28, 1760. This law was not void *ab initio* under the order in council because law passed by the legal authority in the colonies was in force until the royal disapprobation arrived in the colony and was published.[1]

After the statement of the case for the respondents had been made the committee recommended the dismissal of the appeal, which was ordered on December third.[2]

We have now examined the various classes of appeals that were brought from the colonial courts to the King in Council in our second period. It has become evident that the colonies had developed far beyond the previous period. They had tried experiments in the issuance of paper currency and had become involved in matters of finance with the resultant attempts to make adjustments through the usual legal channels. By a review of these cases the home government had been compelled to take a definite stand looking toward the stabilization of this unsettled condition. Other matters of attention were the status of the negro as property in the colonies, the intricate problems connected with American shipping, the status of tobacco as legal tender as well as the dismissal from their positions of persons connected with the religious and educational institutions. The interest was not solely in the procedure but was largely centered in the judicial attitude toward the varying and many-sided life which had developed in the American dependencies. No doubt mistakes were made but the attempt to apply judicially the time honored English legal system to colonial matters introduced a uniformity and a stability in colonial affairs which would not otherwise have been possible.

[1] *British Museum Additional MSS.*, no. 36220, folio 54b.

[2] *Acts Privy Council*, vol. iv, p. 699.

CHAPTER V.

THE WORKING OF THE IMPERIAL SYSTEM

IN the development of the imperial system for the control of the administration of justice the home government was confronted with many problems. These were made more serious because of the time which was evidently necessary to get communications from England to the colonies and receive a reply.[1] Among the more important of the problems from the viewpoint of this study were the creation and administration of the special courts, the question of the tenure of office of the colonial judges, the careful guarding by the English government of its prerogative and the attitude taken by the colonies on this matter together with the consequent obstruction of the working of the imperial system with regard to appeals.

The question of the erection of special courts for the consideration of maritime questions had come up some time previous to 1696. In July of that year the commissioners of the customs had made the following recommendation to the treasury department:

> We move, as highly conducing to the execution of the Acts of Trade and Navigation and for the regulation of the Plantation trade, that Courts of Admiralty may be erected in each colony and that persons of known ability and integrity may be empowered by the Commission of the Admiralty to do their duty therein, and that persons of experience in the laws

[1] Seymour to Board of Trade, May 6, 1701, *CO5/726*, p. 460.

may be nominated by the King and recommended to the Governors as Attorneys-General for the prosecution of bonds, trials of seizures and other matters connected therewith.[1]

Previous to this time maritime questions had been settled in the ordinary law courts and the governor had had admiralty powers defined in his vice admiral's commission which gave him jurisdiction where maritime law was concerned.[2] But it was found upon investigation that no such commissions had been issued to the governors of some of the colonies. Randolph was ordered to attend the Board of Trade and at that time was asked about methods of judicature in the colonies and particularly of "transgressors of Acts of Parliament relating to Trade". He reported to the Board that trials in the ordinary courts of record were commonly very partial and favorable to the transgressors, because both the judges of these courts and juries summoned to serve there were generally men that were themselves interested in the indirect methods of trade. He added that he had himself suffered greatly at the hands of the colonial courts when he had unquestionable right on his side. In his opinion a court of admiralty consisting of a judge, registrar and a marshal together with an attorney-general for the prosecution of causes in the king's name, all to be nominated and commissioned by the king,would be a much better and more effectual method of putting the laws concerning plantation trade into execution than the use of the courts then existing for that purpose. He also said that the appeals from such courts as these should be made easier than from the courts already established there, be-

[1] *Calendar of State Papers, Colonial Series, 1696-1697*, no. 107, pp. 52-53.

[2] Commission to Boone as vice admiral of New Jersey, *New Jersey Documents*, vol. ix, pp. 195-205. *Cf.* Greene, *Provincial Governor*, pp. 105-106; Root, *Pennsylvania*, p. 92.

cause the judges in the colonial courts many times denied writs of appeal and tied up the appellants "by bonds to hard conditions". All this he was asked to put into writing, in order that it might have sufficient consideration.[1]

This report became the basis of the later recommendation of the Board of Trade to the Privy Council for the erection of these special courts.[2] In December, 1696, the Board recommended and the Council issued an order stating that the commissions of vice-admiralty to governors in the colonies should be so made out that in case of a governor's death his power of vice-admiralty should devolve upon his successor.[3] The proprietors and agents now became active and fearing that admiralty courts were about to be erected in their colonies petitioned the king. This petition came from interested persons in the colonies of Carolina, Bahamas, Pennsylvania, East and West Jersey and Connecticut. This stated:

"We observe in the representation of the Council of Trade of December 17 last that notwithstanding our charters, you may appoint courts of admiralty in our provinces and that the Admiralty have reported that all governors of colonies have or might have commissions as vice-admirals. We beg that our governors may have vice-admiral's commissions like the governors of the other plantations."[4]

The evident intention of this was to get the courts into the hands of colonial officials appointed or dependent upon the controlling force in the colony and removed from the im-

[1] Randolph to Board of Trade, *Board of Trade Journal*, vol. ix, p. 25.

[2] *Board of Trade Journal*, vol. ix, p. 291.

[3] *Calendar of State Papers, 1696-1697*, no. 454.

[4] *Calendar of State Papers, 1696-1697* no. 606, p. 314; Nicholson requested Admiralty Courts for Virginia because of the question of piracy. Nicholson to Board of Trade, June 10, 1700, *CO5/311*.

perial prerogative. Soon after, the home government divided the American colonies into vice-admiralty districts. The colonists were now to have courts erected and directed by the imperial forces.

It was under the king's commissions that the colonial vice-admiralty courts were created. These commissions were issued from the high court of admiralty and furnish evidence not only of the jurisdiction of the colonial courts to which they were issued but of the high court of admiralty at home from which they came.[1] The commissions to the governors as vice-admirals were very full, granting in a clear statement an admiralty jurisdiction as wide and beneficial as the most zealous supporters of the English admiralty could ever have wished. The commission to Cornbury of New York as vice-admiral created the courts and gave him the necessary powers of execution. It gave him the powers of vice-admiral " of and in all seas and coasts within your government according to such commission, authorities and instructions as you shall receive from ourself, under the seal of the Admiralty or from our High Admiral or commissioners for executing the office of High Admiral of our foreign plantations for the time being ".[2] In the commissions or letters patent to the governors for the more effectual suppression of piracy it was stated that the governor might preside over an admiralty court for offenses " committed on the sea, or within any harbor, river, creek or place where the admiral had power, authority or jurisdiction ".[3] The commission to Richard Morris as vice-admiralty judge for the district of New York, Connecticut and New Jersey can be taken as showing the extent of the

[1] Bendict, *American Admiralty,* pp. 65-66.

[2] Commission to Cornbury, quoted by Benedict, p. 67.

[3] General Admiralty Commission to Bellomont, *ibid.,* p. 76.

admiralty and maritime jurisdiction in the colonies.[1] The jurisdiction was to extend to all causes, civil and maritime, embracing charter parties, bills of lading, policies of assurance, accounts, debts, exchanges, agreements, complaints, offenses and all matters which in any manner whatsoever relate to freight, transport money, maritime loans, bottomry, trespass, injuries, extortions, demands and affairs whatsoever, civil and maritime. So far as place was concerned it was equally extensive. It was to extend to everything done in, upon, or by the sea or public streams or fresh water ports, rivers, creeks, and places overflown whatsoever within the ebbing and flowing sea or high water mark from all first bridges to the sea.[2] These interpretations were present in the commissions issued and acted under during the whole period of colonial government.

The act of 1696 which erected the courts of admiralty, was rather loosely put together and some difficulties arose almost immediately over it. When a chief justice and attorney general were to be sent to New York in 1700 upon Bellomont's urgent solicitation, it was proposed by a memorial from the Board of Trade that they might be appointed the judge and advocate of the vice-admiralty in the colony. This request was sent by the Board of Trade to the lords of the admiralty. They replied that letters patent of vice-admiralty had been issued to the Earl of Bellomont for the district with the power to appoint deputies and under officers. The Earl of Bellomont had appointed Wade Winthrop and it was not considered necessary to have an advocate as it was an office very seldom, if ever, established in a foreign vice-admiralty.[3] The control of the working

[1] General Admiralty Commission to Bellomont, *ibid.*, p. 82; also *vide* commision to Thomas Boon as vice-admiral of New Jersey in *New Jesey Document*, vol. ix, pp. 196-205.

[2] *Ibid.*, p. 88.

[3] Personal letter of Burchett from the Admiralty office to William Copple, Esq., July 4, 1700. *CO5/1044*, no. 17.

system of the admiralty courts under this act involved problems of jurisdiction, the fee system, the question of appeal to the home government and the decided opposition of the colonists themselves.

There was a conflict between the jurisdiction of the admiralty courts and the courts exercising the common law. The colonists were not slow to see this fact and the crown officials were not able to draw a dividing line. From the court of errors in the colony of New York, the collector and principal officer of the king's customs, Archibald Kennedy, appealed to the Council from a decision which affirmed a former judgment of the court of king's bench in that province. This judgment was one in favor of Thomas Fowles whereby the court of admiralty was restrained from proceeding to determine a suit relating to the seizure of a sloop called *Mary and Margaret* carrying a boat and some merchandise. The question at issue was whether the sloop, having on board commodities of the product and manufacture of Europe, but not shipped in Great Britain, was at the time of seizure on the high seas or within the jurisdiction of New York. At the hearing March 23, 1743, the appeal was dismissed.[1]

Also from the same colony Vincent Pearse appealed from a decision given in the court of errors April 17, 1741, from a similiar judgment of the court of king's bench in favor of George Cummyns, whereby a prohibition was adjudged against the proceeding of the court of admiralty to condemn a vessel called *Restoration,* which was seized by the appellant pursuant to instructions for general reprisals against Spain, as belonging to the subjects of the king of Spain or to persons inhabiting his territory. This time the King in Council reversed both judgments of the New York courts and ordered that a writ of consultation be issued and that

[1] *Acts Privy Council,* vol. iii, no. 538.

the admiralty court be directed to proceed in the original cause. The point at issue was whether at the time of her capture the *Restoration* was lying within the jurisdiction of New York or was on the high seas.[1] A similar reference on the same question was made on an appeal of Captain Pearse with regard to the ship *Canary*, November 19, 1741.[2]

From Rhode Island the owners of a ship *Pearl*, condemned May 6, 1720, in the admiralty court of that province on an information brought by Captain Smart, appealed to have their interest in the *Pearl* proven and to have the sentence reversed and the vessel restored.[3] The case was heard before the committee on March 22, 1723, and here Captain Smart's counsel objected to the Privy Council hearing the case, saying that it did not lie within the jurisdiction of the Council.[4] A postponement was ordered and in July it was recommended that the petition be dismissed without prejudice to the prosecution of an appeal at common law. This conflict between the admiralty courts and the common law courts can also be seen in the development of the admiralty system in Pennsylvania.[5]

A doubt arose as to whether there was any competent jurisdiction for the trial and punishment of persons guilty of murder within the admiralty jurisdiction in the colonies. A Board of Trade representation of March 10, 1762, proposed that a bill with new provisions adapted to such crimes might be prepared. The next day the Board of Trade was ordered by the Council to consult the opinion

[1] *Acts Privy Council*, vol. iii, no. 527.

[2] *Ibid.*, no. 528.

[3] *P. C. 2*, no. 87, p. 360.

[4] *P. C. 2*, no. 88, pp. 280, 330.

[5] *Cf.* Root, *Relations of Pennsylvania with the British Government*, pp. 107-115.

of the law officers of the crown about acts for the punishment of murder and with the advice of the advocate, attorney and solicitor general to prepare a draft of such a bill to be laid before Parliament.[1]

No definite salaries were allowed the officers of the admiralty courts by the home government and this tended to develop the evils of the fee system. Compensation was made upon a basis of a percentage of the cargo condemned. Nathaniel Byfield, a judge of the vice-admiralty court in Massachusetts Bay petitioned the King in Council from a judgment of the superior court at Boston in 1732 reversing a judgment of the inferior court of common pleas upon an action brought by Samuel Swasey, shipwright, against Judge Byfield for "extorsively" taking from him as his fee for his definitive decree twenty shillings more than by the laws of the province was allowed. More than that the judge had condemned him to pay 10 pounds, 40 shillings in bills of credit and the costs of the court.[2] The practice of indiscriminately taking fees was largely influenced by the fact that some of the admiralty judges were customs collectors as well. It became notorious enough by 1776 to get from Burke his denunciation that "a court partaking in the fruits of its own condemnation is a robber".

There was doubt over the question of appeals. The question was raised as to whether appeals were to be heard by the King in Council or the high court of admiralty. This question is early indicated on the part of the colonists and on the part of the home government. On December 18, 1701, the committee for appeals made a representation to the Council touching upon this point. This representa-

[1] *Acts Privy Council,* vol. iv, pp. 530-531.

[2] *Acts Privy Council,* vol. iii, no. 279, p. 384.

tion was referred to the Board of Trade in order that it might send to the governors of the colonies in America for an account of whether the courts of admiralty there were held by virtue of the power given to the governors by the commission which they received from the lords commissioners of the admiralty or by virtue of a clause under the great seal empowering them to erect the courts of admiralty.[1] Previous to this time the Council had established the precedent of receiving appeals from the colonists concerning violation of the trade acts.[2] Jahleel Brenton, the collector, surveyor and "searcher of the customs" of New England, had petitioned the Council December 22, 1692 saying that he had used all lawful means to seize and proceed against all ships and goods brought into the colony contrary to law, but that some persons had taken advantage of the fact that there was no war vessel on the coast and had violated the English law. The Council at this time admitted Mr. Brenton's appeals and decided after some lengthy discussion the question which he brought up for adjudication. This same doubt about appeals is reflected in the Blakiston letter of May 20, 1699, wishing to know whether appeals should go to the high court of admiralty.[3] The attorney general was of the opinion that appeals should be made to the court of admiralty in England.[4] Of the same opinion was Sir Charles Hedges.[5] But the Board saw the inconsistency present in this matter and, while supporting the crown officials in their report, it stated further that it would use

[1] *Acts Privy Council,* vol. ii, p. 303, Dec. 18, 1701.

[2] *Acts Privy Council,* vol. ii, pp. 237-241.

[3] Blakiston to the Board of Trade, May 20, 1699. *CO5/726, vide supra* chapter i.

[4] *CO5/714. Vide supra* chapter ii.

[5] *Ibid.,* no. 74.

its best endeavor to apply such remedies as might be wished by the colonists if a conflict should arise.[1]

Appeals from the admiralty courts were heard by the King in Council despite these opinions. And appeals were also heard by the high court of admiralty in England. The theory was that where the royal commission had given jurisdiction the appeal was to the King in Council, but where the jurisdiction was derived from the admiralty in England then the appeal was to the high court of admiralty. At times an appeal to the King in Council was referred by it to the admiralty. This was true of a petition of one John Smith of New York for relief by letters of reprisals or otherwise for the seizure of his ship *The Three Brothers,* taken, while trading between Jamaica and New York in time of peace, by a French captain and converted to the captain's use. The petition was referred to the admiralty, which reported that the matter involved the eleventh article of the Treaty of Utrecht of 1713 and that this article had not been fully explained. The utmost that could be expected was that the king would renew to his minister in France the demand for the ship and her cargo.[2]

The appeals heard by the King in Council from the admiralty courts were, generally speaking, appeals from unusual decrees in these courts. A group of London merchants appealed July 18, 1700, from a decision of the court of admiralty in South Carolina, which had condemned their ship under the pretence of not having a register and certificate in form as required by law. The committee recommended the admitting of the appeal upon the usual security. In 1701 the owners again petitioned for a speedy hearing and in July of that year the Council reversed the sentence of

[1] Board of Trade to Blakiston, *Calendar State Papers,* vol. x, p. 444.
[2] *Acts Privy Council,* vol. ii, no. 1277, p. 727.

condemnation passed by the Carolina court.[1] Owners of the vessel *Experience and Susanna* appealed in 1701, on the ground that their ship and cargo had been condemned in the admiralty court in Antigua since it was claimed there that the master and three fourths of the crew were not English, whereas the owners claimed that the ship and crew were duly qualified under the navigation acts.[2] The Council reversed the sentence of condemnation passed upon a ship called the *America* in the admiralty court at Antigua. The owner first appealed the case to the high court of admiralty but after was advised to appeal the case to the King in Council which he did in September, 1701. After the Council had given judgment in favor of the owner the judge of the admiralty court refused to order the restoration of the vessel. The case dragged on till July of 1705, when the Council issued an order upon the report of the advocate and attorney general, stating that if difficulty be made about restitution an action should be begun in the dependency for obtaining the vessel, and all the evidence should be found specially in order that the facts might fully appear when there was a further appeal to the king.[3] Officials asked that appeals be dismissed for non-prosecution. An example is furnished by the petition of Matthew Norris of New York April 3, 1735, asking that an appeal of the owners of 401 bags of Spanish snuff and 100 rolls of tobacco condemned as lawful prize be dismissed.[4] John Collins of Maryland, master of the sloop *Patuxent*, appealed from the decision of the court of vice-admiralty in Maryland July 31, 1734, whereby his sloop and goods brought into the court by John Ronsby, the collector of the

[1] *Acts Privy Council*, vol. ii, no. 798.
[2] *Acts Privy Council*, vol. ii, no. 838.
[3] *Acts Privy Council*, vol. ii, no. 839.
[4] *Acts Privy Council*, vol. iii, no. 341.

customs, were forfeited, one third to the crown, one-third to Governor Ogle and one-third to the informer.[1]

There was opposition throughout the colonies, not only to the creation of the admiralty courts, but to their procedure. Rhode Island sought to avoid the imperial control by erecting an admiralty court of her own. An abstract of the law creating the admiralty court together with the statement that although the express words of the charter did not permit the erection of a court of admiralty nevertheless it was thought that the General Council of the Colony had the power of admiralty in the colony in order that "a foundation might be laid to assist His Majesty's subjects in these times of war until His Majesty's pleasure be further known" was sent by the Board of Trade in 1703 to Edward Herlkey, the Attorney General. In a letter to the Board dated December 24, 1703, the attorney general stated that he had considered the abstract, had perused the charter and had found that the "proprietors" would erect courts only for determining all matters happening within that colony, which did not empower them to erect a court of admiralty whose jurisdiction was concerning matters happening on the high seas "which is out of the island". Further he said he could not advise a prosecution against the corporation to make void its charter, because the law was only provisional until the king's pleasure be known.[2] The Rhode Island law establishing the court of admiralty was annulled upon the same opinion with the definite statement that the jurisdiction of the colony extended only to matters within the colony.[3]

From Maryland as early as 1694 a petition was received by the Council which showed the feeling there. This peti-

[1] *Acts Privy Council,* vol. iii, no. 361.

[2] *CO5/1262,* no. 60, enclosure i and ii.

[3] *Acts Privy Council,* vol. ii, p. 457, January 28, 1704.

tion, which was referred to the lords of trade and plantations for report, showed the attitude toward English control and the need for the admiralty jurisdiction. It came from one Rawstone stating that he was a deputy collector of the eastern shore of Maryland and as such seized two vessels which had made no entry. By two of the judges, Henry Darnall and Nicholas Seawell, the ships were taken from him and he was "imprisoned and shamefully abused". He asked that his case be again heard by Governor Nicholson and he might have the liberty to prosecute both Darnall and Seawell.[1]

In 1723 a memorial reached the Council concerning the ill treatment of the judge of the vice-admiralty court in South Carolina. There was also complaint of the contempt of the jurisdiction and authority of the admiralty in that colony by the people, as well as complaint of the little regard which had been shown to the jurisdiction of the admiralty in the other of the king's plantations. The committee reported on this memorial in October, recommending that communication be had at once with the governor of South Carolina and the other governors, in order that no interruption and interference of the courts of vice-admiralty should take place and that they should do their utmost to encourage and support the officers of the vice-admiralty in the just and legal execution of their duty, "so a stop may be put for the future" to those indirect practices of which there had been so much complaint.[2] Later in 1729 the judge of the court of vice-admiralty of North Carolina made complaint to the admiralty of the hardships and interruptions he met with in the execution of his office from the governor as well as from the chief justice. The admiralty sent this to the Council.[3]

[1] *Acts Privy Council,* vol. ii, no. 533; *Calendar State Papers,* vol. ix, 832.

[2] *Acts Privy Council,* vol. iii, no. 50.

[3] *Ibid.,* no. 186.

On April 10, 1730, the admiralty addressed a memorial to the Council concerning the colonial opposition. This requested that directions be given to the governors of the plantations to use their best endeavors to assist the officers of the vice-admiralty courts in all matters that might properly and judicially come under their cognizance. It also asked that the provincial judges should be restrained from interfering with the officers of the vice-admiralty. This memorial had been prepared because of the numerous complaints reaching the home government of the interference of the provincial judges by prohibitions of vice-admiralty proceedings. The committee to whom the matter was referred reported back that the course of justice had been obstructed and that the king's subjects had suffered hardships because of interference with the jurisdiction of the admiralty. It recommended that a set of instructions be issued in order to remove this difficulty.[1]

After the Treaty of Paris of 1763 the English government decided that the condition of things shown by these complaints and memorials should stop. The English admiralty was now in a position to deal with the colonial problems. Consequently, a court of vice-admiralty was established for all the colonies May 18, 1764. A vice-admiral was appointed for the colonies and the vice-admiralty court was to have jurisdiction over all the colonies.[2]

A wail of protest arose from the plantations. It was argued that the inhabitants were now subject to the greatest hardships and intolerable expenses; that the trial by jury which was the privilege of every Englishman was denied; that if a judge could be prevailed upon to certify that there was a probable cause of seizure the claimant was without a remedy; that this was contrary to the practice prevailing

[1] *Ibid.*, no. 205.

[2] 4 George III, ch. 15.

among their fellow subjects in Great Britain.[1] The enlargement of the power and the jurisdiction of the courts of vice-admiralty were now loudly complained of, because the colonists had been rather bitter even against the courts whose authority was circumscribed within moderate territorial jurisdiction. It was stated that a customs official might make a seizure in Georgia of goods ever so legally imported and carry the trial to Halifax 1500 miles distant and that the owner must travel the distance to defend his property. If the judge could be prevailed upon, which it was very well known might too easily be done, to certify a probable cause for the seizure, the owner could not maintain an action for damages against the illegal seizure or obtain any satisfaction other than to return to Georgia quite ruined. From the imperial viewpoint it can be seen, that some measures of tightening the system seemed necessary.[2] It can also be seen that the colonists would never be able to catch this viewpoint, and that the development of hostile feeling was hurrying them toward the American Revolution.

Another special court was the chancery court. The existence of chancery courts was frequently assumed by the English government for the colonies, although they were not established at first in all the colonies, and there was considerable discussion in various provinces over the organization of such courts. Appeals were regularly heard from the chancery courts when they had been organized by the home government.[3]

[1] *Rhode Island Colonial Records,* vol. vi, p. 415.

[2] *Rhode Island Colonial Records,* vol. vi, p. 422.

[3] Chancery Appeals listed through all the volumes, *Acts Privy Council, Colonial Series. Vide* also *British Museum Additional MSS.*, no. 36216, folio 19, the case of Moore *vs* Ford, Barry *et al* from Barbados. Heard at Whitehall June 20, 1726.

Chancery affairs occupied the attention of the home government at various times. The Board of Trade wrote Blakiston in Maryland that divers complaints had been laid before it of the irregularities in the courts of chancery in the king's plantations. It had been reported that in some places the governors and councils sat and acted therein without taking any oath to do equal and impartial justice between the parties concerned in the cases that came before them.[1] Bellomont in 1700 wrote the Board, stating that there was a great want of a court of chancery in New York, but that no one understood the organization of such a court.[2] From Massachusetts one Thomas Newton petitioned the Board, stating that for twenty years past he had been practicing law in that province and that he had had "frequent and sad occasion" to observe the great mischief and inconsistency that happened because of the want of an established court of chancery. The courts of the colony gave no relief in cases of trusts, redemption of mortgages, accounts and other such matters cognizable in such courts. He then cited instances which would prove his case.[3]

There was a division of opinion between the home government and the colonists over the question of the tenure of office of the judges. The home government insisted that judges should be appointed during pleasure by the governor and council, while the colonists stood firmly for appointment during good behavior. The argument of the colonists was that the methods used in the reign of King James to

[1] Board of Trade letter to Blakiston, August 20, 1701. *CO5/726*, pp. 95-97.

[2] Bellomont to Board of Trade, October 17, 1700. *CO5/1045*, no. 1.

[3] Letter and memorial of Thomas Newton of Boston to the Board of Trade, received March 29, 1706. *CO5/864*, no. 54. Newton cites instances in Massachusetts legal history in which the want of a chancery court is shown.

make the judges countenance his arbitrary proceedings and the abuses that followed upon it showed the Parliament in the following reign the necessity of putting it out of the power of the government to displace any judge but for official misbehavior.[1] The assembly in the colony of Pennsylvania went on record as stating that, though the governor should appoint judges, they should be displaced for misbehavior at the request of the assembly.[2] In other words, no objection was raised to the appointment of judges by the governors, but when guilty of official misbehavior they were to be removed by the assembly.

Pennsylvania and North Carolina passed laws providing for tenure during good behavior in 1759 and 1760 respectively.[3] Both these laws were disallowed. In 1761 the Council requested of the lieutenant governor of New York that commissions be granted to judges during good behavior. This was referred to the home government in no uncertain terms. With this representation the committee heartily agreed in its report of November 21, 1761, and the Council issued an order that instructions be sent to the various colonies in accordance with it.[4]

The Board of Trade representation of November 11, 1761, in this New York case stated the position of the Board on this question of tenure. It showed that the king's instructions to all the governors in America had said that judges were to be appointed during pleasure only. The cases between the mother country and the colonies were in no degree similar. The change which the tenure of the commission of the judges underwent at the time of the reve-

[1] *Penn. Col. Records,* vol ii, p. 313.

[2] *Penn. Col. Records,* vol. ii, p. 267.

[3] See Greene, *Provincial Governor,* p. 135.

[4] *Acts Privy Council,* vol. iv, no. 460, p. 494.

lution in England was founded upon the most conclusive and repeated proofs of arbitrary and illegal injustice under the influence of the crown. This circumstance did not exist in the American colonies, because the governors were frequently obliged to appoint such persons as offered themselves for amongst the inhabitants, however unqualified they were, though a more fit person might afterward be found. If the commission were during good behavior, the unqualified person could not be displaced. The representation closed with the statement that the policy of appointment during good behavior was considered by the lords commissioners "as subversive of all true policy, destructive to the interests of Your Majesty's subjects and tending to lessen that just dependence which the colonies ought to have upon the government of the mother country".[1]

The Board was then directed to prepare a draft of instructions. These were reported back to the Council on December 2 and the next day approved by the Council. These instructions were issued to all the governors of the American colonies containing directions carrying out the policy enunciated in the original report with respect to the tenure of the commissions to be granted by the governors to the chief judges and the justices of the courts of judicature in the colonies. This, however, did not settle the issue as is indicated in that clause of the Declaration of Independence which says that the king "has made judges dependent on his will alone for the tenure of their offices."

The home government jealously guarded its prerogative in other ways. Acts passed in 1699 and 1701 in New Hampshire with regard to the establishment of courts were repealed by the Council in 1706. The recommendation of the Board of Trade had stated that both acts encroached upon the

[1] *Acts Privy Council*, vol. iv, pp. 499-500; *Board of Trade Journal*, vol. 69, p. 348.

royal prerogative. The first act was repealed because it prevented appeals if the value involved was less than three hundred pounds; these the crown should be permitted to allow if it wished. The second act was dissallowed because the legislation did not state that appeals to the Council were allowed.[1] Acts passed by the colonial assemblies, which extended the jurisdiction of the inferior courts, were repealed by the Council.[2] In South Carolina a law of 1720 was declared null and void, the Board of Trade giving the reason that it had been passed by a revolutionary body. This act encroached upon the royal prerogative by the provision that the governor, council and assembly should hear appeals in cases involving more than one hundred pounds and that where more than five hundred pounds were involved appeals might be made to the King in Council.[3] In Pennsylvania there was a long period of dispute between the colony and the home government after the passage of Pennsylvania's first judiciary act of 1701. The acts of 1701, 1711, 1715 and 1722 all received the royal veto because, in the organization of the judicial system for the colony, the scheme did not meet with the approval of the English authorities.[4]

The colonists, however, would not always admit the claims of the imperial government with regard to the judicial system. This was particularly true in the case of appeals to the King in Council from the New England

[1] *Laws of New Hampshire*, vol. i, pp. 661, 862.

[2] *North Carolina Colonial Records*, vol. ix, pp. 619, 670. Jackson reported the repeal of these acts not only because of the extension of jurisdiction but also because of a clause giving an attachment against the goods of persons.

[3] *Cf.* Smith, *South Carolina as a Royal Province*, 1719-1776, pp. 122-125.

[4] Root, *Relations of Pennsylvania with the British Government*, chapter 6; see particularly pp. 158-174.

colonies. Bellomont wrote to England during the years 1699-1700 concerning the attitude of the New England colonies toward appeals. In a letter to the Board of Trade November 28, 1700, he spoke of the refusal on the part of New Hampshire and Boston to allow appeals in two specific cases and added that he did not doubt that in both cases the Board "will make an inquisition why appeals were refused these parties".[1] From Rhode Island Dudley wrote the Board at great length under date of November 2, 1705, stating that proceedings in the courts of justice were arbitrary and unjust, and as the eighth of the grievances which he listed he stated that the colony had refused to allow appeals to the home government and gave "great vexation to those that demand the same". He enclosed in this report affidavits to prove the correctness of his complaint.[2] The Brinley case had drawn the definitive statement from the home government that appeal was the inherent right of Englishmen.[3] The Palmes case in Connecticut drew attention to that colony and led to a similar statement there.[4] Even Virginia was accused of preventing appeals.[5] The attitude of Massachusetts was extremely hostile, as is indicated by the "New England Address about Appeals," dated March 25, 1698.[6] But as the eighteenth century advanced the opposition died down gradually until there was scarcely anything to be found in the way of open refusal of appeal.

The Massachusetts government refused the appeal of one

[1] Bellomont to Board of Trade, November 28, 1700. *Co5/1045*, no. 18.

[2] Report of Dudley to Board of Trade concerning irregularities in Rhde Island, November 2, 1705. *CO5/1263*, pt. 2 with enclosures.

[3] See *supra* chapter i; *Acts Privy Council*, vol, ii, 732.

[4] See *supra* chapter i.

[5] *Calendar State Papers*, vol. x, p. 657.

[6] See *supra* chapter i; *CO5/860*.

George Lawson to the King in Council from a sentence given in the inferior court of common pleas at Boston in 1704 and confirmed the same year in the superior court in favor of Peter Sergiant. The petition, however, was heard despite the action of Massachusetts and in 1706 the committee recommended that the governor of Massachusetts state the reasons for refusing to admit the appeal and forward all papers relating to the case and that all parties should attend the first meeting of the Council in November prepared to be heard.[1] The judges of the superior court of Massachusetts answered the order in council, October 2, 1706, pointing out that the refusal of Mr. Lawson's appeal was because the sum involved was under three hundred pounds.[2] In May, 1707, the committee recommended the dismissal of the case which was ordered by the Council. This case is cited as an indication of the attempt on the part of the Privy Council to be fair and judicially minded.

There were instances of evasion of the decrees of the King in Council. The conspicuous case of the colonial period is that of Leighton *v* Frost.[3] In the Freebody case from Rhode Island, appealed to the Council in 1766, but still under discussion in 1771, an order had been issued concerning the computation of interest. The superior court of Rhode Island evaded the issue presented by the order in council and Freebody petitioned a second time. The committee ordered the judges of the superior court to return an answer within three months. On the committee report of July 6, 1774, after counsel had been heard on both sides, peremptory order was given to the judges of the colonial court to comply with the orders in council of 1769.[4]

[1] *Acts Privy Council,* vol. ii, no. 990.

[2] *Board of Trade Journals,* 1704-1709, p. 324.

[3] *See supra* chapter III.

[4] *Acts Privy Council,* vol. v, pp. 24-25.

Three cases are usually cited as involving the validity of colonial legislative enactments and a diligent search of the records yields no more. These cases are Winthrop *v* Lechmere from Connecticut; Phillips *v.* Savage from Massachusetts; and Clarke *v.* Tousey, also from Connecticut.

John Winthrop of New London in Connecticut petitioned January 16, 1727, for permission to appeal from two sentences of the superior court of Connecticut in favor of Thomas and Anne Lechmere relating to the real estate left the petitioner by his ancestors, and that an act passed by the assembly of Connecticut empowering Thomas Lechmere to dispose of the property might be repealed.[1] The facts in the case showed that General Wait Winthrop died intestate, leaving two children, John Winthrop and Ann, the wife of Thomas Lechmere of Boston, a merchant. John Winthrop was made executor of the estate and did not make any inventory or account of his administration. In July, 1724, Lechmere applied to the court of probate insisting that he was in right of his wife entitled to a proportion of the estate, but that he was kept from it because Winthrop had not inventoried or administered the same. Lechmere caused Winthrop to be summoned before the court of probate and there Winthrop maintained that he was the heir at law and was in possession of the estate by his right of inheritance under the common law of England. Consequently, he was not obliged to give an account of the real estate belonging to his father. Lechmere was wishing to establish a claim to one third of the estate under a Connecticut law passed in 1699 concerning the distribu-

[1] *Acts Privy Council,* vol. iii, no. 112, pp. 139-171; *Connecticut Colonial Records,* vol. vii, pp. 571-579; *Connecticut Historical Society Collections,*—vol. v; Andrews, The Connecticut Intestacy Law—*Yale Review,* vol. iii, p 261; Dickerson, *American Colonial Government,* pp. 274-277; Schlesinger, Colonial Appeals to the Privy Council, *Political Science Quarterly,* vol. xxviii, pp. 440-446.

tion of intestates. This law had provided that the real estate of an intestate was to be divided so that a double portion went to the eldest son. This was in opposition to English common law by which the whole of an estate passed to the eldest son.

The case was in the Connecticut courts until March 22, 1726 when on an appeal in review the letters of administration granted Winthrop were vacated and the administration of the estate given to Thomas and Ann Lechmere. Appeal was denied Winthrop in the Connecticut courts but upon his petition to the King in Council he was admitted to an appeal. The hearing before the committee was held December 20, 1727. The respondents advanced the fact of the Connecticut legislation and the appellant attempted to show that the Connecticut law was contrary to established law in England. Winthrop definitely asked that "His Majesty would repeal" an act passed by the Assembly empowering Lechmere to sell and dispose of Winthrop's real estate and would restore to him his father's estate.

The verdict was given by the Council upon recommendation of the committee in favor of Winthrop. This seems to have been due largely to the skill of his attorneys, Yorke and Talbot.[1] The Connecticut law was declared to be null and void because it was contrary to the laws of England and because it made lands of inheritance distributable as personal estates and was not warranted by the charter of the colony.[2]

Previous to the passage of the Connecticut law of 1699, Massachusetts had passed an act for the distribution of estates of intestates. An appeal reached the King in Council, calling in question this colonial statute as contrary to English common law, in the case of Phillips *v* Savage.[3]

[1] *Vide* Dickerson, *American Colonial Government*, p. 275.

[2] *Acts Privy Council*, vol. iii, p. 149.

[3] Phillips *v* Savage, *Acts Privy Council*, vol. iii, no. 322; *P. C. 2*, no. 93, pp. 95, 101, 166, 186. *P. C. 2*, no. 94, pp. 203, 267, 353, 374. *Mass. Lower House Journal*, December 14, 1738, p. 35.

The petition of Gillam Phillips of Boston, the son and heir of Henry Phillips, gentleman, of Boston for an appeal from an order of the governor and council of Massachusetts Bay, November 3, 1733, approving of a division of the real estate of his brother among his mother, sister and himself pursuant to the orders of the judge of the probate of wills, was referred to the committee November 7, 1734. The appeal was admitted in February of the following year. On July 22, 1737, Samuel Wilks, the agent of the colony, addressed a memorial to the committee, setting forth that the judgment from which Phillips was appealing was founded upon a general law of Massachusetts for the settling of estates which had been constantly observed and put into practice since the law had been passed and had obtained the royal approbation. He asked that the validity of this law might in no way be called in question but that if it was the general court of the province might be heard by their counsel in support of the bill. This shows the consternation that seized the Massachusetts people when it was thought that the council might impeach the force or validity of the law.

The committee heard the case and the arguments of the counsel in December, 1737, and in January, 1738. Here the appellant represented that he was, by the common law of the realm, solely entitled to the estate of his brother and that no act of the province of Massachusetts could vary the common law of the realm or change or alter the course of descent. The legislation of the Massachusetts assembly was therefore null and void for want of power in the assembly to enact such legislation. Upon this the appellant had refused to distribute the intestate's real estate. The estate had been divided into five parts by order of the judge of the probate of wills and Gileam Phillips had appealed to the governor and council of the province. But the governor and council had upheld the probate court. The appellant had then asked for an appeal to the king, but this had been refused by the Massachusetts authorities.

The committee reported that the act of the Massachusetts Assembly had been passed as long before as the year 1692 and had been ratified and confirmed in 1695 by the then lords justices in council. Several other acts in addition to and explanatory of it had been passed in Massachusetts, one as late as 1731, and the records of the colony showed that estates had been distributed according to these acts. Therefore, the committee recommended that the divisions of the estate stand, the judgments of the Massachusetts courts be affirmed and the appeal dismissed. This was done by an order in council of February 15, 1738.

The question of the intestacy laws came up again in an appeal from Connecticut. This was in the appeal of Samuel Clark of Connecticut in 1737 from a sentence of the superior court in March 1733 in favor of Thomas Tousey, Esq., and Hannah, his wife, together with four other persons, concerning the distribution of land.[1] This land had belonged to the estate of Samuel Clark, Esq., deceased, and again called into question the law passed by the Connecticut assembly concerning the estate of intestates. The colony itself was so vitally interested that it helped by money expenditures to assist in the appeal. The appeal was admitted May 25, 1738, and a second one May 17, 1742. On July 4, 1745, the case was heard before the committee and on its recommendation, July 18th of the same year, the peti-

[1] Clark *v* Towsey et al. *Acts Privy Council,* vol. iii, no. 422, pp. 580-581. *Connecticut Colonial Records,* vol. viii, pp. 506-507; Andrews, Connecticut Intestacy Law, *Yale Review* iii, pp. 2661-264; Schlesinger, Colonial Appeals to Privy Council. *Political Science Quartery,* vol. xxviii, p. 445; Hazeltine, Appeals from Colonial Courts, *Am. Hist. Review,* 1894, pp. 319-320.

tion was dismissed, the judgments of the lower courts affirmed and the validity of the Connecticut act concerning the estates of intestates sanctioned which reversed the former decision enunciated in the appeal in the case of Winthrop *vs* Lechmere.

It has been generally supposed that during the colonial period no great constitutional importance was attached to these decisions declaring a colonial statute contrary or in accordance with established English law. As a matter of fact there is evidence to show that legal authorities both in the colonies and in England saw the importance of the precedent which had been established.[1] The King in Council was at once an executive and a judicial body. In its executive capacity the Privy Council passed upon, and when necessary, disallowed colonial legislation. When a

[1] In the plea of John Camm before the general court of Virginia at Williamsburg, April 10, 1764, in the case of Camm *v.* Charles Hansford and William Moss in which a Virginia statute was involved this statement was made:

> "A noble Lord of great weight in the Council declared that if the validity of the act had come before them in an appeal touchiny any dispute concerning it (the Virginia act) they must have declared it no law from its manfest injustice, if there had been no other objection to it." *Bitish Museum Additional Mss.* 36220, folio 53.

Later, when the case reached the Privy Council on the appeal of John Camm, the attorneys, Norton and Willes, offer, as part of the plea of the appellant in the hearing before the committee, November 27, 1765 the following statement:

> "For that acts have, upon the hearing of private appeals been declared void, particularly the Privy Council, on hearing an appeal between Winthrop and Lechmere from Connecticut in 1727 judicially declared two acts of assembly passed in that province void; the one a general one, to make lands descendible to all the children; the other a private one, to take away the administration from Winthrop who refused to exhibit an inventory and to give it to Lechmere, who would exhibit one". *Ibid.*, folio 54.

judicial hearing called in question this legislation it was only natural that the Council should express itself upon the validity of it. As the early American jurists began to develop their ideas of jurisprudence it might have been expected that they would follow this precedent. In this sense this function of the Privy Council became the precedent for that power of judicial annulment of legislation exercised at the present time in the United States by the Supreme Court.

BIBLIOGRAPHICAL NOTE

No bibliographical list accompanies this monograph as the results are based largely upon the source material found in the British Museum and the Public Record Office in London. Following the example of other persons who have used this material I have listed it under the call number used at the Museum and the Record Office. Where secondary material has been used it has been specifically cited in the foot notes.

At the Public Record Office the most important material for this work is found in the manuscript records of the Board of Trade and the original records of the Privy Council. The original papers and the entry books are listed here under the citation of the Public Record Office as C. O. Following this comes the number of the classification, the number of the volume and, where it is possible, the number of the manuscript within the volume. Much use has been made also of the eighty-four volumes of the Board of Trade Journal, a record of the proceedings at the Board meetings, valuable principally as an index to the other manuscript papers. Generally speaking, the Acts of the Privy Council, Colonial Series, vols. 1-5, together with the Calendar of State Papers, Colonial Series, America and West Indies, have been used for the actions of the Privy Council. However, in cases where use has been made of the original Privy Council Register, a valuable record kept with the greatest of care explaining the relation between the Board of Trade and the Privy Council, it is listed under the call number of the Record Office, namely P. C. 2.

At the British Museum are to be found the briefs in Privy Council appeals between the years 1752 and 1769 in the so-called Hardwicke Papers, British Museum Additional Manuscripts 36217-36220, listed in this monograph under manuscript and folio number. These are a series of briefs, including those of the first Earl of Hardwicke when he was known as Sir Philip Yorke, with his notes after his accession to the bench and briefs with the notes of his son, the Honorable Charles Yorke. Sir Philip Yorke, after a splendid career as a solicitor became solicitor-general in 1720, chief justice in 1733 and was created Baron Hardwicke of Hardwicke in Gloucestershire. He retained the chief justiceship until June 8, 1737, when he became lord chancellor. Charles Yorke, the second son of Lord Chancellor Hardwicke, was likewise a solicitor of great brilliance and became lord chancellor in 1770. He was attorney in a number of cases coming on appeal from the colonies.

It is unfortunate that the sources do not give us more complete and accurate information concerning final decisions reached by the King in Council and the discussions at the meetings of the committee on appeals. Reference is made to colonial petitions with no further mention concerning them in the Privy Council Register. Our only sources of knowledge concerning the discussions at the meetings of the committee are the scant statements which sometimes appear with the record of the final decision or the scribbled notes found on the lawyer's briefs. It would have been interesting to follow the line of reasoning by which the committee arrived at its recommendations.

In secondary material there are two excellent monographs of importance concerning appeals. These are H. D. Hazeltine's, "Appeals from the Colonial Courts to the King in Council with Especial Reference to Rhode Island," *Annual Reports of the American Historical Association*, 1894, pp. 299-350 and A. M. Schlesinger's "Colonial Appeals to the Privy Council," *Political Science Quarterly*, vol. xxviii, pp. 279-297, 433-450. Indebtedness is gratefully acknowledged to both of these studies.

CPSIA information can be obtained
at www.ICGtesting.com
Printed in the USA
BVHW080328090722
641521BV00002B/195

9 781616 192501